RAND EDUCATION

T0302770

Promoting the Long-Term Sustainability and Viability of Universities in the Pennsylvania State System of Higher Education

Charles A. Goldman, Rita Karam, Mark Stalczynski, Katheryn Giglio

Prepared for the Pennsylvania Legislative Budget and Finance Committee
Approved for public release; distribution unlimited

For more information on this publication, visit www.rand.org/t/RR2486

Library of Congress Cataloging-in-Publication Data

ISBN: 978-1-9774-0063-5

Published by the RAND Corporation, Santa Monica, Calif.

© Copyright 2018 The Pennsylvania Legislative Budget and Finance Committee

RAND® is a registered trademark.

Cover: Monkey Business / Adobe Stock.

Support RAND
Make a tax-deductible charitable contribution at
www.rand.org/giving/contribute

www.rand.org

Preface

The Pennsylvania Legislative Budget and Finance Committee, a committee of the Pennsylvania General Assembly, sponsored a RAND Corporation study to identify options that would improve the long-term sustainability and viability of the universities in the Pennsylvania State System of Higher Education (State System) in the coming years. The State System was established in 1982 and is the largest provider of higher education in the Commonwealth of Pennsylvania. Today, the State System faces considerable challenges that threaten the sustainability of its operations and the provision of accessible, affordable, and relevant educational programs to students.

Based on the study, this report documents the main external and internal challenges faced by State System universities and analyzes five possible options that could address those challenges to at least some extent. The report also highlights implementation implications for each option and concludes with a recommended option.

We expect this work to be of interest to the Pennsylvania General Assembly; officials of State System, state-related, and private higher education institutions; and the Pennsylvania public. It should also be informative to those in other states that might be facing similar challenges.

This research was conducted by RAND Education, a division of the RAND Corporation, with funding from the Pennsylvania General Assembly's Legislative Finance and Budget Committee. For more about RAND Education, visit www.rand.org/education.

Table of Contents

Preface.. iii

Figures... vi

Tables... vii

Summary.. viii

    External and Internal Challenges and Effects on State System Institutions and Students.................... viii

    Effects of Challenges on Institutions and Students...xii

    Options for Change xiii

    Recommendations xvii

Acknowledgments... xviii

Abbreviations xix

CHAPTER ONE

Introduction... 1

    Study Approach..2

    Background: State System 2

    Background: Higher Education in Pennsylvania 3

    Organization of This Report...5

CHAPTER TWO

Challenges Arising from External Factors.. 6

    Demographic Changes Suggest a Decline in the Number of State High School Graduates....................6

    State Financial Support Is Limited...10

    Universities in the State Face Strong Competition 12

CHAPTER THREE

Challenges Arising from the System 14

    State System Governance Structure Sometimes Allows Political Concerns to Outweigh System
        Needs 14

    Governance Structure Is Bureaucratic and Does Not Promote Accountability 15

    Cumbersome State Rules Reportedly Add Costs and Delays 18

    System Office Support and Services Do Not Always Meet the Needs of Individual Institutions 19

    Faculty Labor Relations Limit Flexibility..19

    State System Universities Focus on Limited Markets 22

CHAPTER FOUR

Consequences of Internal and External Challenges for State System Universities and
        Students... 26

    Consequences for Institutions 26

    Consequences for Students..31

CHAPTER FIVE

Options to Address Challenges 36

    Objectives Guided the Development of Options 36

    Broad Strategies for Change 37

    Options for Change 38

    Evaluating the Prospects for the Options 46

    Should the Commonwealth Establish a Statewide Body to Coordinate or Oversee Higher
        Education? 47

CHAPTER SIX

Conclusion and Recommendations 49

APPENDIX A

Study Approach 51

APPENDIX B

Detailed Tables and Graphs 53

    Financial Indicators 63

APPENDIX C

Response of the State System's Interim Chancellor 74

References 77

Figures

S.1. Forecast Change in Youth Population by County, 2015–2030 ix

S.2. Major Sources of State System University Revenues as a Share of Total, 2006–2016 x

S.3. Change in Net Position (Surplus or Deficit), Three-Year Average at State System
Universities, 2006–2008 to 2014–2016 xii

1.1. Five Study Tasks 2

1.2. Location of State System Universities 3

2.1. Pennsylvania High School Graduates, Actual (2005–2015), and Projected (2016–2030) 7

2.2. Forecast Change in Youth Population by County, 2015–2030 8

2.3. Major General Fund Appropriations for Higher Education in Pennsylvania, 2007–2017 10

2.4. Major General Fund Appropriations for Higher Education in Pennsylvania, by Type,
2007–2017 11

2.5. Major Sources of State System University Revenues as a Share of Total, 2006–2016 12

2.6. Location of State System and State-Related Universities in Pennsylvania 13

4.1. Change in Student Enrollments (Fall FTE) at State System Universities, 2010–2016 27

4.2. Change in Net Position (Surplus or Deficit), Three-Year Average at State System
Universities, 2006–2008 to 2014–2016 30

4.3. Median Tuition and Mandatory Fees for In-State Students, by Sector, 2007–2016 32

4.4. Median On-Campus Room and Board, by Sector, 2007–2016 33

4.5. Six-Year Graduation Rates by Sector, with National Averages, 2016 34

4.6. Six-Year Graduation Rates at State System Universities, 2016 35

B.1. Location of State System and State-Related Universities in Pennsylvania 58

B.2. Estimated Cash Flow, Three-Year Average at State System Universities, 2006–2008
to 2014–2016 64

B.3. Ratio of Estimated Cash Flow to Long-Term Debt, Three-Year Average at State
System Universities, 2006–2008 to 2014–2016 65

B.4. Ratio of Estimated Long-Term Debt to Total Revenues, Three-Year Average at State
System Universities, 2006–2008 to 2014–2016 66

Tables

1.1. Pennsylvania Postsecondary Institutions and Students Enrolled, 2016 4

2.1. Forecast Change in Youth Population by University Enrollment Regions, 2015–2030 9

3.1. Students by Level and Sector, 2016 23

3.2. Percentage of First-Time Undergraduate Students from Outside Pennsylvania,
2006–2016 23

3.3. Change in Total Degrees Awarded by Broad Field and Sector, 2010–2016 (percentage) 24

3.4. Distance Education Students as a Percentage of Total Enrollment by Sector, 2012–2016 ... 25

3.5. Distance Education Students as a Percentage of Total Enrollment at State System
Universities, 2012–2016 25

4.1. Student Enrollments (Fall FTE) at State System Universities, 2010–2016 27

4.2. Students and Staff by Sector, 2010 and 2016 28

4.3. Change in Students and Staffing at State System Universities, 2010–2016 29

B.1. Projected Population by County, Age 15–19 Years, Pennsylvania, 2015–2030 (Sorted
in Descending Order of Growth) 53

B.2. State System University Enrollment Areas and Projected Population Change, Ages
15–19 Years, 2015–2030 55

B.3. Total Degrees Awarded by Broad Field and Sector, 2006–2016 59

B.4. Undergraduate In-State Tuition and Fees by Sector ($), 2007–2016 61

B.5. On Campus Room and Board by Sector ($), 2007–2016 61

B.6. Six-Year Graduation Rates by Sector and National Averages, 2006 and 2016
(percentage) 62

B.7. Six-Year Graduation Rates at State System Universities, 2006 and 2016 (percentage) 62

B.8. Students and Staffing at State System Universities, 2010–2016 63

B.9. Change in Net Position (Surplus or Deficit), Three-Year Average at State System
Universities, 2006–2008 to 2014–2016 ($million) 67

B.10. Estimated Cash Flow, Three-Year Average at State System Universities, 2006–2008
to 2014–2016 ($million) 67

B.11. Ratio of Estimated Cash Flow to Long-Term Debt, Three-Year Average at State
System Universities, 2006–2008 to 2014–2016 (percentage) 68

B.12. Ratio of Estimated Long-Term Debt to Total Revenues, Three-Year Average at State
System Universities, 2006–2008 to 2014–2016 (percentage) 68

B.13. Faculty Contract Provisions, Pennsylvania and Selected Other States 69

Summary

The Pennsylvania State System of Higher Education (State System) is the largest provider of higher education in the Commonwealth of Pennsylvania and has worked since 1982 to provide accessible, affordable, and relevant undergraduate, graduate, and career-development programs to the public. State System institutions are owned by the state, but the state also supports other institutions, including community colleges, private institutions, and four state-related universities.

Today, the State System faces considerable challenges that threaten the sustainability of its operations. The State System commissioned the National Center for Higher Education Management System (NCHEMS) to assess these challenges and recommend solutions (NCHEMS, 2017). Following NCHEMS's report, the Pennsylvania Legislative Budget and Finance Committee, a committee of the Pennsylvania General Assembly (the state's legislature), contracted with the RAND Corporation to look beyond the scope of the NCHEMS study by developing and analyzing possible courses of action that would increase sustainability for the universities in the system.

In this report, we document our analysis of the challenges that State System and its universities face, and we propose and analyze five options that state decisionmakers might choose from in determining next steps. Quantitative data collected for this work was supplemented with documentation, interviews, visits to State System university campuses, and reviews of other states' higher education policies and governance structures.

External and Internal Challenges and Effects on State System Institutions and Students

The challenges that State System universities face are of a dual nature. On one hand, external factors—such as declining college enrollment and state support, as well as increasing competition from other higher learning institutions—are challenges faced by many university systems across the United States. On the other hand, the State System and its universities face several unique internal challenges, such as the system's governance structure.

External Challenges

Pennsylvania's declining traditional college-age population: Most of the State System universities serve a local area and draw students from surrounding counties as well as the Philadelphia and Pittsburgh regions. All but ten counties in Pennsylvania are expected to experience a decline in traditional college-age population (and seven of these exceptions are very small counties). This will likely present significant challenges to most of the State System universities. Figure S.1 shows youth population projections between 2015 and 2030 and the locations of State System universities. The green shades indicate growing counties. The orange shades indicate declines, with darker shades indicating larger projected declines. As the figure shows, most of the map is orange.

Figure S.1. Forecast Change in Youth Population by County, 2015–2030

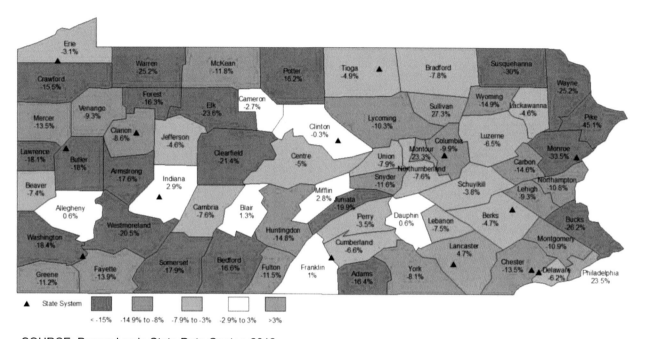

SOURCE: Pennsylvania State Data Center, 2012.
NOTE: This map reflects population projections of 15- to 19-year-olds.

Limited state support: Pennsylvania provides a low level of public financial support for public higher education compared with other states. State appropriations for higher education declined sharply in 2011–2012 following the Great Recession, and cuts were not distributed evenly across all types of higher education in the commonwealth, with the largest ones applied to the state-related institutions. As a result, appropriations have accounted for a smaller proportion of State System university revenues; tuition and fees make up a larger proportion. These are illustrated in Figure S.2.

Competition among colleges and universities in the area: In interviews, State System university officials reported that competition for students is intensifying. Many noted that this is partly because of the decrease in the traditional-age college student population. They also cited competition with state-related university branch campuses, which benefit from state funding but operate under considerable autonomy from the state compared with the State System.

Figure S.2. Major Sources of State System University Revenues as a Share of Total, 2006–2016

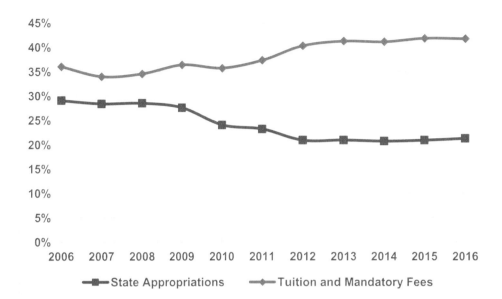

SOURCE: RAND calculations from National Center for Education Statistics, undated.
NOTE: Not all sources of revenue shown.

Internal Challenges

Governance that can place politics above system needs: State System and university officials reported that the State System governance structure sometimes allows political views, rather than the best interests of the system and its universities, to govern decisions. A Board of Governors that oversees the State System includes the governor and several members of the legislature representing partisan points of view. This structure enables members to infuse their ideologies and views in education discussions.

Interviewees also noted that board members serve simultaneously on various Councils of Trustees at State System institutions. These councils have significant duties related to appointments and institutional policies and programs, including contracts, fees, and budgets. It should be noted that issues pertaining to political governance are related to Act 188 of 1982 (Commonwealth of Pennsylvania, 2016), the founding legislation of the State System, and changing the structure of these groups would require legislative action.

Bureaucratic governance: As defined by Act 188, the roles and responsibilities of the Board of Governors, the Chancellor's Office, university presidents, and Councils of Trustees overlap in some areas. For example, the approval of academic programs requires the review and authorization of both the Board of Governors and the Councils of Trustees (with the board recently delegating its authority to the Chancellor's Office). In other areas, the legislation is ambiguous. For example, Act 188 lacks clarity in defining the decision authority held by the Board of Governors and the Chancellor's Office.

This increases bureaucracy and weakens efforts to hold the institutions accountable. Public higher education systems in California and Maine do not have Councils of Trustees or any other governing structure at the institutional level that adds extra layers of authority.

Limited chancellor authority: Act 188 limits the chancellor's capacity to address the challenges facing the system and his or her ability to hold institutions accountable. A critical area where the chancellor does not have adequate power is in negotiation of collective bargaining agreements. This power rests with the board to a substantial extent, and the membership and structure of the board leaves it vulnerable to the influence of the statewide faculty union.

Cumbersome state rules: State System universities are state-owned and thus must deal with regulatory state rules and oversight pertaining to procurement and construction. These rules are much more stringent than those dealt with by state-related universities. According to interviewees, rules and regulations related to the threshold part of Act 188, the Administrative Code, the Procurement Code, the Commonwealth Attorneys Act, and the Separations Act all add layers of bureaucracy and remove contract-related independence from universities. These rules also add costs and slow down institutional efforts to purchase services and improve facilities.

Inadequate system office support and services: Although the State System Office offers shared services and contracts, a number of interviewees from individual State System institutions suggested that the office does not provide needed support, such as back-office services or consolidated contracts for food services, to assist individual institutions and reduce their costs. Furthermore, institutional leaders reported that different parts of the system office ask for information, often to check compliance, and these different requests overlap in what they request. Institutional leaders also reported that the system office does not use the information it receives to offer strategic advice to help universities improve their performance.

Inflexible faculty labor relations: Interviewees from all sides of State System institutions reported a stressed relationship with the statewide faculty union. Factors said to be contributing to this strained relationship include contract provisions and their enactment and the collective bargaining agreement negotiation process. In addition, restrictive language pertaining to faculty, adjuncts, and staff are seen as hindering academic program restructuring efforts and responses to current challenges.

Focus on limited markets: State System universities focus mostly on in-state undergraduate education. The State System's traditional concentration in education degrees has posed a major challenge as enrollments in this field have declined markedly statewide. In addition, while a few universities are using distance education to reach working students and those who live outside their region, most of these efforts have few students enrolled entirely in distance education, leaving the universities dependent on serving students in their local region.

Effects of Challenges on Institutions and Students

The challenges we have described are already affecting State System universities in negative ways and will continue to do so. First, the 14 universities have already experienced a 12.9-percent decline in enrollment between 2010 and 2016. Moreover, shrinking state support, fewer enrollments, and other factors have created a situation in which some State System universities are experiencing significant financial stress and others are heading in that direction. Figure S.3 graphs the three-year average of surpluses or deficits. Each cluster of bars represents the 14 State System universities for one three-year period (ending in the year marked). In the early years, most universities show surpluses. During the Great Recession, a few universities show deficits in each period. In the most recent three years, the pattern changes significantly. More universities are experiencing deficits over time and fewer surpluses. Some parts of the pattern in the last year or two represented in Figure S.3 likely stem from 2015 changes in governmental accounting standards that require public universities to record long-term liabilities for retiree pension benefits.

Figure S.3. Change in Net Position (Surplus or Deficit), Three-Year Average at State System Universities, 2006–2008 to 2014–2016

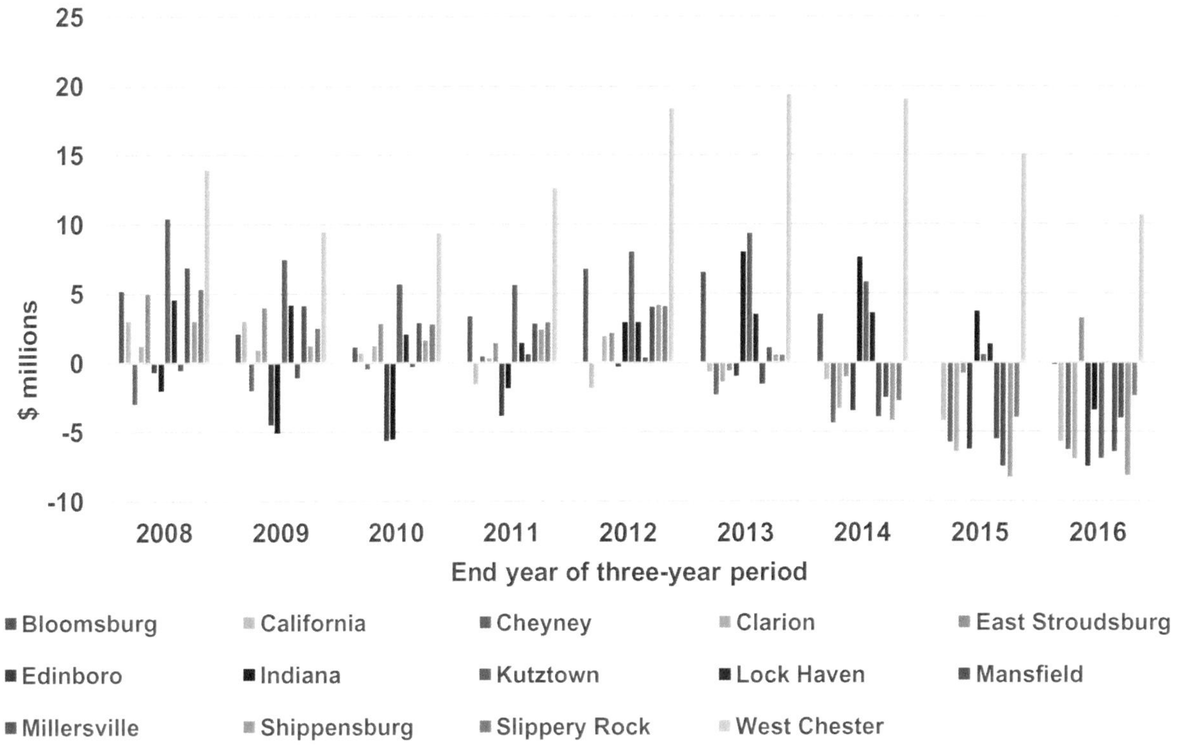

SOURCE: RAND calculations from National Center for Education Statistics, undated.
NOTE: Each bar represents one of the 14 State System universities, shown in alphabetical order. All adjustments to net position, such as one-time changes in liabilities, are excluded.

Nonetheless, the trend prior to this change in 2015 and the overall pattern indicate reason for concern about deficits.

These challenges will likely affect students. Right now, State System tuition levels remain more affordable than those of state-related institutions. However, room and board charges are increasing faster than at competing institutions, reaching a level equal to state-related institutions—and they could continue to rise. Moreover, some services, such as counseling and student retention initiatives, have been curtailed while others have been downsized, with staff let go or asked to reduce hours. These services are critical to ensure the success of students, particularly underrepresented and first-generation students. Interviewees suggested that inadequate state support and revenue from tuition have affected these providers of student support, as has increased competition for funding among the different services. Finally, while State System graduation rates are slightly above the national average, with 56.6 percent of students graduating in six years, graduation rates for state-related and four-year private institutions are higher compared with both national averages and the State System. These differences could reflect a different mix of students and their needs—and, possibly, better academic and student services offered at state-related and private institutions.

Options for Change

Based on our analysis of the current situation and goals expressed in stakeholder interviews, we developed six objectives to guide the development of options:

1. Strengthen financially weak institutions.
2. Adjust the size of campus facilities and staffing to match enrollments.
3. Restructure programs for greater efficiency and responsiveness to enrollment trends.
4. Maintain access to college education for Pennsylvanians at an affordable price.
5. Preserve the historic mission and identity of current universities.
6. Avoid difficult implementation requirements.

It is probably not feasible to meet all six objectives fully, but this list can serve as a useful way to compare the options we develop and highlight the trade-offs that various options entail.

There are five options to consider. These range from maintaining the system structure with some changes to merging the universities with one or more state-related universities.

Option 1: Keep Broad State System Structure, Including Current Individual Universities, but with Improvements

Under this option, the State System's overall governance structure, the State System functions, and individual institutions missions are preserved. This upgrades the existing system to a certain extent by modifying its current governance structure, reallocating authority so it is more balanced across the various system levels, and relieving institutions from some state requirements, such as those for procurement and construction.

To achieve this goal, the option requires amendments to Act 188.

Implementation considerations for Option 1 include the following:

- **Modify the Board of Governors membership to reduce political influence and conflicts of interest in the decisionmaking process of the State System**. This could be accomplished by changing the composition of the board so that it is better equipped to represent the interests and needs of the state and its diverse regions.

- **Eliminate the Councils of Trustees.** The councils add another layer of bureaucracy because they are tasked with reviewing and approving institutional policies, programs, and budgets.

- **Institutions, upon their own discretion, could establish an advisory board.** This group would offer support to the institution's administrators and faculty, provide input from key stakeholders regarding strategic direction, guide quality and program improvement, and assess program relevancy in relation to the labor market.

- **Enhance the authority of the chancellor and provide more leeway to respond to challenges**. A larger leadership role for the chancellor would include evaluating the performance of presidents and institutions and holding them accountable, providing support to struggling universities, providing recommendations to the Board of Governors regarding institutional budgets, and requiring institutions to share services.

- **Adopt a graduated autonomy approach for the presidents of institutions.** Institutions that demonstrate healthy enrollment and finances should be granted greater autonomy to manage themselves; struggling institutions should be subject to greater oversight.

- **Provide the institutions with more independence and freedom in how they conduct their contracts and procurement.** Relieve the institutions from the contractual and procurement constraints they have because of being state-owned.

Although these provisions do not change the faculty labor agreements in any direct way, a less political board with clearer authorities for it, the chancellor and the university presidents could lead to an improved relationship between the faculty union and the State System, where the union and system negotiate contracts that provide greater flexibility in managing the faculty workforce.

Option 2: Keep Broad State System Structure with Improvements Accompanied by Regional Mergers of Universities

This preserves the state system's overall governance structure and the State System's functions but consolidates the current 14 universities into a smaller number, perhaps ranging from five to eight. As with Option 1, the system will be upgraded by modifying its current governance structure. However, under this option, weaker State System institutions will be merged into those that are fiscally viable. Act 188 will need to be amended.

Implementation considerations for Option 2 include the following:

- **Understand the short-term costs of mergers**. It could be that mergers are costly in the short term but might save the system a significant amount of money in the long run. Since 2010, there have been more than 40 mergers across nine states with mixed results regarding cost savings.
- **Address debt**: The State System or the state should assist the fiscally viable institutions with taking on the debt incurred by the fiscally weak institutions.
- **Modify labor agreements**: The State System and the faculty union will have to restructure contract terms to accommodate the combination of faculty across merged institutions.
- **Establish committees across merged institutions**. A committee representing the merged institutions could work collaboratively with the chancellor to determine which programs should continue and the basis on which faculty and staff members should be retained or let go.
- **Coordinate mergers with accreditation agencies**. Mergers will require endorsement from accreditors to extend the universities' separate accreditations to accreditation for the combined entity.

Option 3: Merge State System Universities and Convert to State-Related Status

Under this option, the State System structure would be eliminated and universities would convert to state-related status. Independence is not recommended for universities that are struggling or facing significant market challenges; this option could be applied only to the stronger universities or to weaker universities that could be merged with stronger ones prior to independence.

To implement this option, several of the implementation steps of Option 2 are required: The debt the institutions have accrued needs to be addressed by the state, and labor agreements will require revision to reflect the merged institutions. Merged institutions need to establish committees to address which programs to continue and staff to retain, and mergers also need to be coordinated with accreditation agencies.

Implementation considerations for Option 3 include the following:

- **Repeal Act 188**. This step will need to be taken so that the institutions are released from their state-owned designation.
- **Create legal bindings**. Mergers should be enacted into law and the merged universities established as state-related institutions.
- **Establish legislation if a state coordinating board is selected**. Create legislation that provides specific authorities for the coordinating board.

- **Consider bonds**. The merged universities can take on primary obligation for repaying bonds issued by the former universities. The state might have to offer a guarantee for bonds in the event of default by the new universities because the State System is being eliminated.

Option 4: Place the State System Under the Management of a State-Related University

Under this option, the State System and all its institutions come under the management by a large state-related university, building on its strong performance. This option preserves all institutions as they currently stand: their institutional missions and accreditation, state support, labor union relations, and faculty contracts. The main change would be in governance and operations. The Board of Governors would be accountable to the governing body of the state-related university while the state-related university will oversee personnel, business functions, and procurement. It could provide a shared service model for business operations and support.

Implementation considerations for Option 4 include the following:

- **Evaluate risk level**. The state-related university would need a due diligence period to more deeply assess debt levels, finances, and levels of risk before adopting this option.
- **Modify Act 188 pertaining to the governance structure**. Board selection and assignment and contract and procurement regulations need to be modified through legislation.
- **Ensure state funding commitment**. This arrangement should include a dissolution option in the event that state support does not continue.
- **Put in place short-term and long-term plans regarding this arrangement**. The state-related institution should assume this role for a defined period, after which it will assess the successes or failures and decide whether to continue the arrangement. The state should be ready to intervene and support institutions if the arrangement is not to be continued.

Option 5: Merge State System Universities into State-Related Universities

Rather than try to improve current governance arrangements or replace them with new arrangements, a final option is to build on the strong performance of the state-related universities by merging State System universities into one or more of the state-related universities.

Implementation considerations for Option 5 include the following:

- **Repeal Act 188 if no universities will remain in the State System.**
- **Plan a transition path for employee labor relations**. State-related universities do not have collective bargaining for most employees, so the merged institutions will require a transition plan for integrating employees with or without collective bargaining.
- **Coordinate institutional mergers with accreditors.**

- **Enact institutional mergers in law**. This option would require that all assets be given to the state-related parent institution, which would also accept all liabilities.
- **Consider bonds.** Because the State System is being eliminated, the state might have to offer a guarantee for bonds in the event of default by the state-related universities.

Recommendations

The challenges facing the State System and its universities are serious. Since many of the challenges arise from demographic and financial trends outside the control of higher education institutions, we do not think that changing the structure and relationships within the State System (Option 1) is likely to address the long-term challenges sufficiently.

Given the considerable uncertainties entailed in all the options, especially Options 2–5, we cannot be sure which option has the strongest chance to make the current universities more sustainable. Based on the limited prospects we see for Option 1, we think the state should seriously consider other structural change options. These options are likely to be more difficult to implement and could entail other risks, including possible increases in student costs and the loss of valuable sovereign immunity from lawsuits that protects current State System universities. But if they are implemented well, these options are likely to meet the key objectives of strengthening financially weak institutions and better matching staffing size to enrollment trends.

At this stage, we do not know if the large state-related institutions would be seriously interested in Option 4 (state-related control) or Option 5 (merger as branch campuses) or if they would have a preference for one option over the other. We think these two options have the best long-term prospects and recommend either of them, if one or more willing partners can be found among the state-related institutions.

If the state and one or more large state-related institutions cannot reach an agreement to implement either Option 4 or 5, the state then should consider mergers, such as Options 2 or 3. It appears feasible to use more than one of these options, rather than treating all 14 current State System universities the same. For instance, some stronger State System universities could be made independent, while weaker ones could be merged into stronger State System or state-related universities as branch campuses.

Although mergers are risky because they often entail considerable friction and costs to implement, they have long-term potential to make universities more flexible and responsive to trends in enrollments.

Finally, the state could theoretically benefit from a coordinating body to align the activities of its diverse set of higher education providers. But because of our concerns about the additional layers of bureaucracy and difficulty in getting political support from the major higher education sectors, we advise against establishing such a body unless it is necessary for a specific purpose under one of the options selected here, such as a body to distribute state higher education funding according to an agreed formula.

Acknowledgments

We thank the staff of the Pennsylvania General Assembly's Legislative Budget and Finance Committee, led by two executive directors over the course of this project, Philip Durgin and Patricia Berger. These directors and staff assisted us throughout the study with guidance on the legislature's interests in the study, access to information, and introductions to stakeholders. We also appreciate the thoughtful responses to our inquiries for interviews and data sources from many officials in the State System, its universities, and the state-related universities.

We are grateful for the careful reviews of this report by Darleen Opfer, Fatih Unlu, Grace Evans, Jayme Fuglesten, Brian Pusser, and Jason Lane. We also appreciate the research assistance of Diogo Prosdocimi and the careful editing of Arwen Bicknell.

Abbreviations

CO	Chancellor's Office
COT	Council of Trustees
FTE	full-time equivalent
IPEDS	Integrated Postsecondary Education Data System
NCHEMS	National Center for Higher Education Management Systems
Penn State	Pennsylvania State University
PHEAA	Pennsylvania Higher Education Assistance Agency
Pitt	University of Pittsburgh
State System	Pennsylvania State System of Higher Education

Chapter One

Introduction

The Pennsylvania State System of Higher Education (State System), formed in 1982 by Act 188 of the General Assembly (Commonwealth of Pennsylvania, 2016), has strived to provide accessible, affordable, and relevant undergraduate, graduate, and career-development programs to the commonwealth. Today, the State System is the largest provider of higher education in Pennsylvania. The system comprises 14 university campuses, four branch campuses, and several off-campus instructional centers, and it serves approximately 105,000 students, 88 percent of whom are state residents. The State System is also the 12th-largest employer in the state, employing about 12,000 faculty and staff per year.

Like many state higher education systems today, the State System faces significant challenges. The Pennsylvania General Assembly has repeatedly expressed concern about the State System and proposed to commission a study on options available to aid Pennsylvania's higher education system. While the legislature was considering a resolution to commission such a study, the State System commissioned a study by the National Center for Higher Education Management Systems (NCHEMS). In July 2017, NCHEMS released its study and corroborated several growing concerns within the commonwealth that the State System and its institutions are experiencing extreme stress because of declining enrollment and fewer financial resources (NCHEMS, 2017). Following the release of the NCHEMS report, the legislature revised its resolution and commissioned a second study through the Legislative Budget and Finance Committee, which was awarded to the RAND Corporation.

Our team framed three primary questions derived from the language that the Pennsylvania General Assembly provided in Senate Resolution 34 of 2017 (General Assembly of Pennsylvania, 2017):

1. What are the most-promising options to help the universities in the State System become more sustainable and better able to manage the allocation of scarce state financial resources?
2. What are the strengths, weaknesses, implementation requirements, and challenges of the most promising options?
3. How could a new or restructured state entity exercise responsibility for policy coordination and leadership across all postsecondary institutions in the commonwealth? What benefits does such an entity offer to the commonwealth and its institutions?

This report documents findings and recommendations related to these three questions. More specifically, it reexamines the challenges that the State System faces and in response, develops and assesses five courses of action and describes what is needed to implement each one. This work should be of interest to the General Assembly, State System officials, and other interested stakeholders committed to the State System's near- and long-term success.

Study Approach

To develop feasible options for the universities in the State System, the study team needed to fully understand the system's challenges, its guiding policies and structure, and the way that other states' higher education systems have addressed or are addressing similar challenges. Moreover, options needed to be developed and assessed in relation to feasible outcomes and implementation necessities. The study was thus conducted in five interrelated steps which are illustrated in Figure 1.1 and described in greater detail in Appendix A.

Figure 1.1. Five Study Tasks

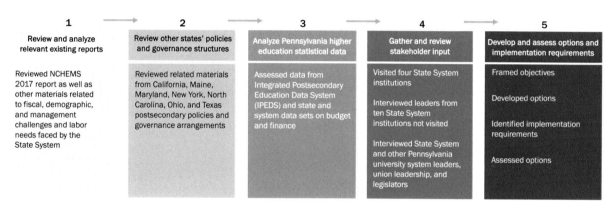

NOTE: Integrated Postsecondary Education Data System (IPEDS) data is gathered by the National Center for Education Statistics, undated.

Background: State System

The State System was formed in 1982 by Act 188 of the General Assembly, bringing together 14 state-owned universities, most of which had developed from the state's historic teacher training colleges.

The State System is governed by the Board of Governors, which appoints the system chancellor. The board and chancellor exercise substantial control over policies for the system and for individual universities, although each university is independently accredited and led by a president. Each individual university has a Council of Trustees (COT), which oversees a number of functions related to the university, such as approval of new academic programs, approval of campus fees, review of budgets and contracts, providing advice to the system on the performance of its president, and recommending two candidates for the Board of Governors to consider when appointing a new president.

2

Only two State System universities (West Chester and Cheyney, both in the Philadelphia suburbs) are located in a major metropolitan area of the state. The rest, as shown in Figure 1.2, are located in small cities and rural areas around the state.

Figure 1.2. Location of State System Universities

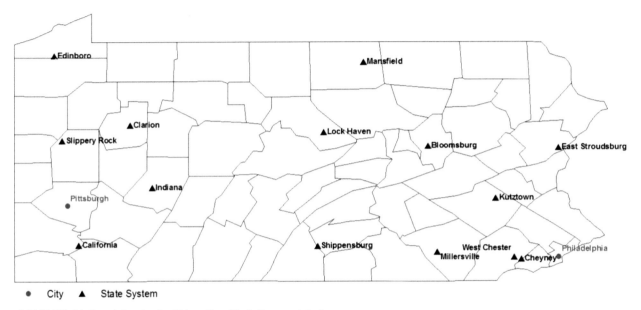

● City ▲ State System

SOURCE: National Center for Education Statistics, undated.

Background: Higher Education in Pennsylvania

Pennsylvania has a wide range of postsecondary education providers, many of which receive some form of public support.

The postsecondary sectors include the following:

- **The State System's 14 state-owned universities:** The State System's 14 universities (and their four branch campuses) are owned by the state. The State System receives funding from a state appropriation under a privileged status requiring a simple majority vote in the General Assembly.

- **State-related:** The state also supports four universities that are not considered state-owned and enjoy considerably more autonomy from the state than the State System. These include Lincoln University, Pennsylvania State University (Penn State), University of Pittsburgh (Pitt), Temple University, and the branch campuses and affiliates of these institutions. These universities receive funding from state appropriations under a nonprivileged status requiring a two-thirds majority vote.

- **Four-year private:** These include private institutions classified as baccalaureate, master's, and doctoral/research institutions (according to Carnegie code) that are comparable to State System universities. These institutions and their students could receive funding from the state through Pennsylvania Higher Education Assistance Agency (PHEAA).

- **Community colleges:** These include 14 public community colleges that offer associate's degrees and receive funding from a state appropriation, as well as the Thaddeus Stevens College of Technology, which also receives funding from a separate state appropriation.
- **Specialized:** These include specialized public and private two-year institutions (e.g., business, cosmetology) and specialized private four-year institutions (e.g. seminary, chiropractic, design).

For the rest of this report, we compare a series of indicators for the first four sectors listed above: State System, state-related, four-year private, and community colleges. We do not include the specialized institutions in these comparisons because their specialized nature leads them to be less similar to and less competitive with State System universities.

Table 1.1 provides a general overview of the postsecondary institutions in Pennsylvania. There are 113 general-purpose four-year colleges and universities, 15 community colleges, and 237 specialized institutions. (The State System and state-related figures in the table include the total number of distinct main campuses, branch campuses, and affiliates for each university.) In the table and in much of this report, we present student enrollments in estimated full-time equivalents (FTEs), which we calculate by adding Fall full-time students to part-time students, with part-time students prorated using standard IPEDS factors for the average fraction of time that part-time students are enrolled.

Table 1.1. Pennsylvania Postsecondary Institutions and Students Enrolled, 2016

Type of Institution	Number of Institutions	Students (Fall FTE)
State System	18	93,848
State-related	33	158,319
Four-year private	66	219,562
Subtotal four-year general institutions	113	471,729
Community colleges	15	70,924
Specialized	237	75,297
Total	365	617,949

SOURCE: National Center for Education Statistics, undated.

In addition to the state appropriations that go to specific institutions, the PHEAA is funded by the commonwealth to provide grants to students attending public and private institutions in the state. It also provides institutional grants to private institutions that enroll students receiving PHEAA grants.

Organization of This Report

This report describes the results of an objective, external evaluation of challenges facing the State System universities, with a focus on the development of feasible structural and management options that could meet current challenges. In Chapters Two and Three, we present findings related to external and internal factors, including demographic changes, state funding and resources, current governance and support structures, and labor union expectations. Chapter Four describes how the external and internal factors described in Chapters Two and Three coalesce into significant challenges for management, faculty and staff, and students. Chapter Five presents five options for consideration, including maintaining the current structure with some changes, different institutional-level mergers, and a combination of options. This chapter also describes the key requirements to implement each of the options described, assesses the prospects of each option to address the challenges facing the universities in the State System, and considers whether the state should add a state-level coordinating body. Finally, Chapter Six summarizes key findings and offers recommendations for the General Assembly, higher education leadership, and other stakeholders to consider. Appendixes A and B provide additional information on the study methods and a set of detailed tables and figures to support the analysis in the main body of the report.

We shared draft and final copies of this report with the State System's Interim Chancellor. The interim chancellor's response to the report is provided in Appendix C.

Chapter Two

Challenges Arising from External Factors

This chapter provides an overview of key external factors that currently and will continue to challenge the sustainability of the universities in the State System in the current configuration. We discuss the ways in which demographic changes will affect the number of enrolled students and how declining state financial support, in combination with fewer tuition-paying students, will continue to limit the State System's ability to fulfill its mission. This chapter also considers the competition that the State System faces in attracting students from the state and from nearby New York, which recently enacted a free tuition policy for middle-class state residents. These three challenges—declining enrollment, declining state support, and increasing competition—will need to be addressed by the plan of action decisionmakers choose to pursue.

Demographic Changes Suggest a Decline in the Number of State High School Graduates

As the NCHEMS analysis makes clear, most of the State System universities serve a local area and draw students from surrounding counties. Some universities also draw from the Philadelphia and Pittsburgh regions. Pennsylvania is anticipated to continue to experience a decline in its traditional college-age population. While universities might maintain or even increase enrollments by retaining students at higher rates or enrolling them from less traditional markets, these demographic changes present significant challenges to most of the State System universities.

The number of students graduating from Pennsylvania's high school graduation cohort rose steadily for about 15 years, from the mid-1990s to 2010. As depicted in Figure 2.1, high school graduation classes have started to decline from those high points and are projected to decline further through 2030 (and beyond, although not shown in the graph).

Figure 2.1. Pennsylvania High School Graduates, Actual (2005–2015), and Projected (2016–2030)

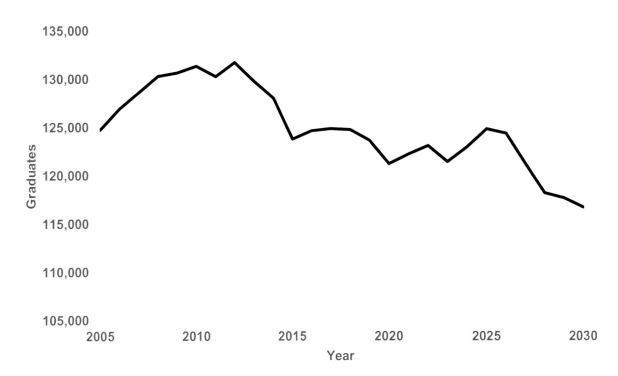

SOURCE: State System Chancellor's Office (CO).
NOTE: Vertical axis does not extend to zero in order to highlight variation.

Looking at the projections between 2015 and 2030 summarized in Figure 2.2, the shades indicate projected growth or decline in youth population. We chose to use Pennsylvania State Data Center (2012) projections for the age group encompassing 15- to 19-year-olds because the projections are available in five-year groups and this group most closely matches the population that is making choices about college. These projections are used by state agencies and in the state budget for planning purposes.

In the map, green indicates projected growing counties. The white shades indicate counties where youth population appears level. The orange shades indicate declines, with darker shades indicating larger projected declines. Most of the map is orange—55 of the 67 counties are projected to experience declines in youth population of between 3 percent and 45 percent over this 15-year period. Youth populations in eight counties are projected to remain fairly steady (defined as growth or decline of less than 3 percent). Only four counties are projected to see a growing youth population and two of these counties are very small. Thus, the only significant growth in youth population is expected in two counties: Philadelphia and Lancaster. Furthermore, while the urban Philadelphia county is projected to see some growth, the entire Philadelphia metropolitan area, including the surrounding suburban counties, is expected to be about level (–0.1 percent change). Appendix Table B.1 provides a more detailed look at the data presented in the figure.

7

Figure 2.2. Forecast Change in Youth Population by County, 2015–2030

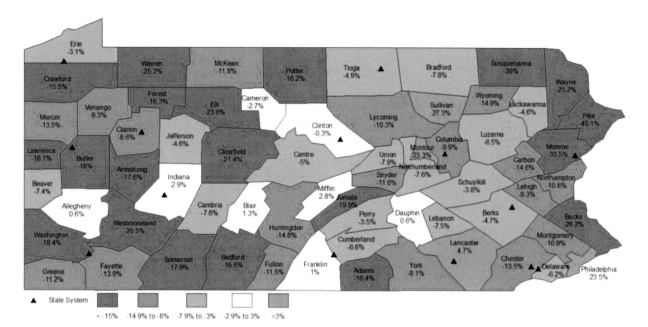

SOURCE: Pennsylvania State Data Center, 2012.
NOTE: This map reflects population projections of 15- to 19-year-olds.

State System Enrollment Will Likely Be Affected by Demographic Changes

As already noted, State System universities primarily serve in-state traditional-age students and typically attract students from a regional county area surrounding the university. In addition, a number of the universities draw significant enrollment from either the Philadelphia metropolitan area, the Pittsburgh metropolitan area, or both. Thus, these demographic changes represent significant challenges. Looking more specifically at the traditional market for each university, we estimated the youth population growth or decline in the counties that each university typically draws from.

Appendix Table B.2 provides detailed projections for each university using the Fall 2016 county enrollment patterns from the State System Chancellor's Office (CO) and the latest youth population projections from the Pennsylvania State Data Center (2012) for the counties that feed each university. Table 2.1 summarizes anticipated youth population changes in three areas: (1) the regional county area that the university currently draws from (based on 2016 enrollment patterns), (2) the Philadelphia metropolitan area, if that is a current source, and (3) the Pittsburgh metropolitan area, if that is a current source. To avoid double counting in the table, only the metropolitan area is shown if the university's regional county area overlaps with one of the two metropolitan areas. Appendix Table B.2 shows the specific regional county areas in these cases.

Table 2.1. Forecast Change in Youth Population by University Enrollment Regions, 2015–2030

University	Regional County Area	Philadelphia Metropolitan Area	Pittsburgh Metropolitan Area
Bloomsburg	−8.2	−0.1	N/A
California	N/A	N/A	−7.6
Cheyney	N/A	−0.1	N/A
Clarion	−8.8	N/A	−7.6
East Stroudsburg	−26.0	−0.1	N/A
Edinboro	−5.4	N/A	−7.6
Indiana	−0.5	−0.1	−7.6
Kutztown	−6.6	−0.1	N/A
Lock Haven	−8.3	−0.1	N/A
Mansfield	−6.8	−0.1	N/A
Millersville	1.4	−0.1	N/A
Shippensburg	−3.3	−0.1	N/A
Slippery Rock	N/A	N/A	−7.6
West Chester	N/A	−0.1	N/A

SOURCE: RAND calculations from enrollment regions from the CO and projections in Pennsylvania State Data Center, 2012.

NOTE: Columns indicate forecast change in population ages 15 to 19 for areas that contribute significantly to current enrollment at each university. N/A indicates that the area is not a significant source of current enrollments for that university based on university enrollments by county in 2016. N/A is also shown for regional county areas where the university's regional area overlaps substantially with one of the two metropolitan areas shown.

Table 2.1 demonstrates that only one university (Millersville) draws from a region expected to have a growing youth population through 2030. Aside from Millersville, the most favorable situation is in the Philadelphia metropolitan area, with roughly level youth population. This metropolitan area is the primary region for Cheyney and West Chester. In total, then, three universities are facing roughly level demographics, and the other 11 all face a shrinking youth population in their traditional enrollment areas.

Demographics are also changing the composition of enrollment. Student enrollments at all types of institutions in the state are becoming more racially and ethnically diverse. In 2016, the State System enrolled 16 percent of its Fall FTE undergraduates from the underrepresented minorities of African Americans and Hispanics, an increase of 5 percentage points from just six years earlier. The State System enrolls a higher percentage of these students than the state-related or four-year private sectors, which each enrolled 14 percent from these groups in 2016. These sectors have also experienced increases since 2010, although those increases have been more modest than the State System has experienced (National Center for Education Statistics, undated).

State Financial Support Is Limited

The availability of public funding presents another challenge. Pennsylvania provides a low level of public financial support for public higher education compared with other states (NCHEMS, 2017). The Great Recession severely challenged state budgets, including that of Pennsylvania. While federal stimulus funding supported some state appropriations for a few years during and right after the recession, appropriations for higher education declined sharply in 2012 and have changed little since then (see Figure 2.3). These cuts were not distributed evenly across all higher education sectors in the commonwealth. Figure 2.4 displays the major appropriations in four categories (and excludes certain minor categories). It shows that the largest cuts were applied to state-related institutions and PHEAA. PHEAA has been able to generate income by servicing student loans and thus to generally maintain available funding for student and institutional grants.

Figure 2.3. Major General Fund Appropriations for Higher Education in Pennsylvania, 2007–2017

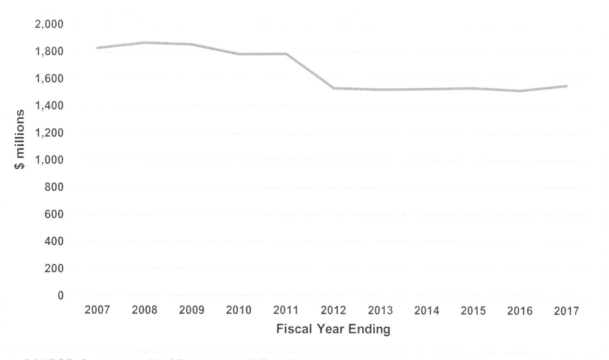

SOURCE: Commonwealth of Pennsylvania Office of the Budget, 2018.

The State System's appropriation declined after 2009 and has only recently begun to increase somewhat. None of these figures are adjusted for inflation, so even a level rate of funding implies that state funding would make up a diminishing share of institutional budgets, as we explore further in Chapter Four.

Figure 2.4. Major General Fund Appropriations for Higher Education in Pennsylvania, by Type, 2007–2017

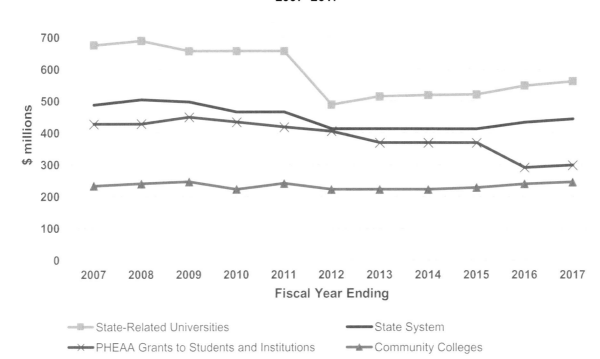

SOURCE: Commonwealth of Pennsylvania Office of the Budget, 2018.
NOTE: The community colleges measure includes appropriations for Thaddeus Stevens College of Technology but excludes annual transfers of approximately $50 million to the Community College Capital Fund. Other, smaller appropriations for higher education within the Department of Education and the Higher Education Assistance Agency are not included.

As a result of these changes, state appropriations are accounting for a smaller proportion of State System university revenues while tuition and fees are accounting for a larger proportion, as shown in Figure 2.5. Over the period from 2006 to 2016, state appropriations fell from 29 percent of total revenues to 21 percent, while tuition and mandatory fees increased from 36 percent to 42 percent. (In making this calculation, we include auxiliary revenues, such as housing and dining, in the total revenue base but do not include their charges in the tuition and mandatory fees.)

Economic situations and budget priorities shift over time, so perhaps the General Assembly will decide to devote more funding to higher education in the future. But the projected declines in the state's youth population and significant increases in older population are often associated with increased pressure on state budgets for health care and other services rather than education. As a result of these long-term trends, we are not confident that the state will decide to allocate significantly more public funding to higher education in general or to the State System in particular.

Figure 2.5. Major Sources of State System University Revenues as a Share of Total, 2006–2016

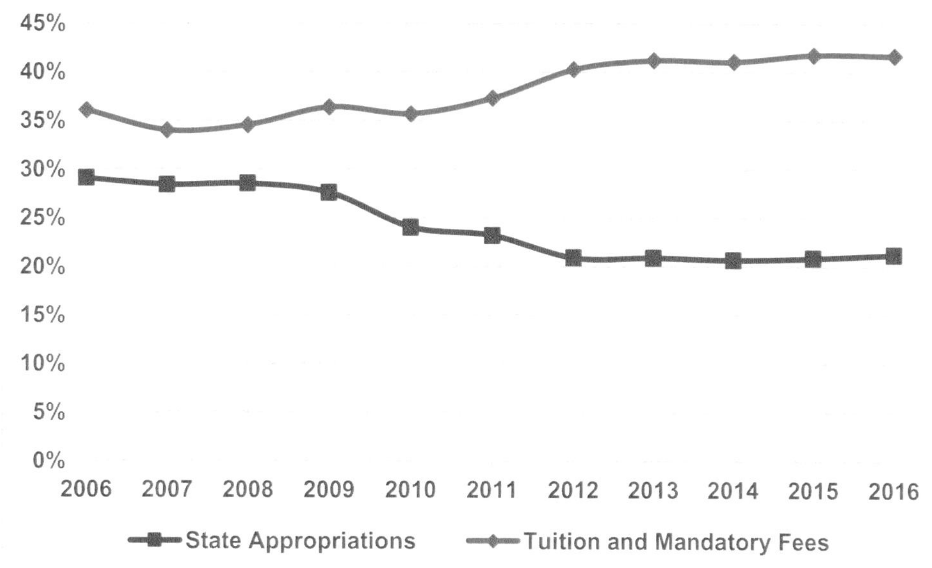

SOURCE: National Center for Education Statistics, undated.
NOTE: Not all sources of revenue shown.

Universities in the State Face Strong Competition

Pennsylvania has many postsecondary institutions, especially for a state of its size. The NCHEMS analysis concluded that Pennsylvania has:

- the 13th-highest concentration of postsecondary institutions relative to population among all 50 states (ranking states by the ratio of institutions to population)
- the fourth-highest concentration among states with more than 500,000 residents ages 18–34
- the fourth-highest concentration of private postsecondary institutions compared with population among all 50 states. (NCHEMS, 2017, p. 9).

As a result of the large number of institutions and the diminishing pool of traditional-age students in the state, officials at State System universities reported that competition for students is intensifying. State System university officials frequently cited branch campuses of Penn State and Pitt as competitors for students in their region. The locations of the state-related main and branch campuses are shown in relation to the State System universities in Figure 2.6. In many regions of the state, both State System and state-related institutions are available to students. (In Appendix B, Figure B.1 provides the same map with each county labeled for reference.)

Competition with other states for student enrollments is expected to intensify. As is the case in Pennsylvania, projections indicate that most surrounding states—specifically Ohio, New York, New Jersey, and West Virginia—are also expected to see declines in their numbers of high school graduates (Bransberger and Michelau, 2016). Other factors also could increase competition for students. For example, the recently enacted New York State Excelsior

Scholarship promises free tuition at public colleges and universities throughout that state for New York families earning up to $125,000 per year (New York State, undated). Officials at State System universities, especially those that typically enroll students from New York, reported that they expect fewer such students to attend in the future.

Figure 2.6. Location of State System and State-Related Universities in Pennsylvania

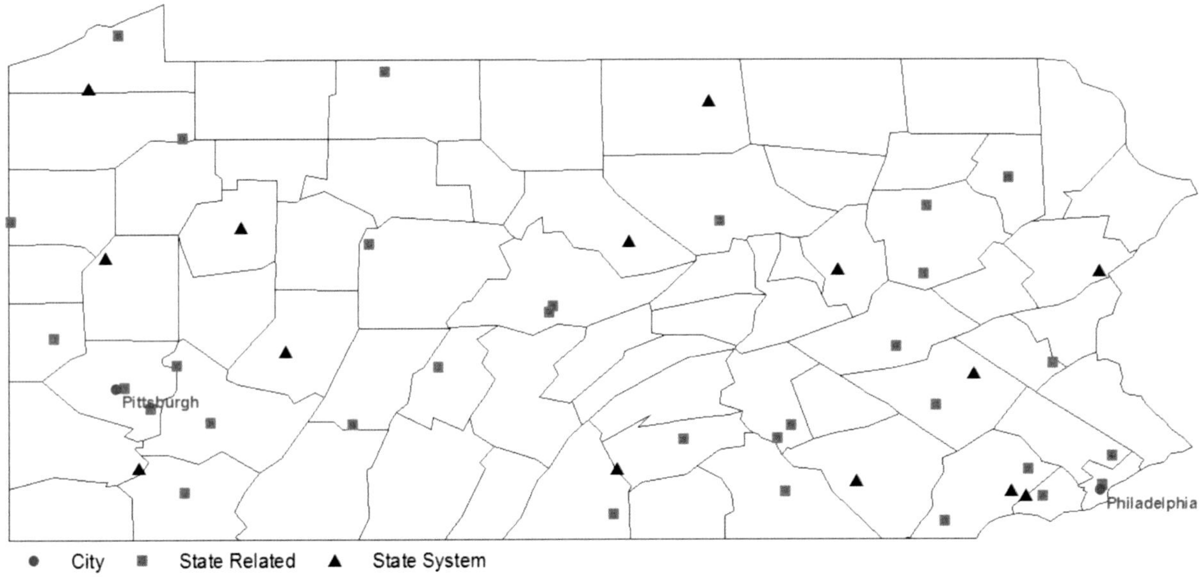

SOURCE: National Center for Education Statistics, undated.

Chapter Three

Challenges Arising from the System

In this chapter, we describe the key system-related factors that challenge the sustainability of the State System and are likely to continue to do so. We discuss the complex political nature of State System governance, supporting the findings of the 2017 NCHEMS analysis but also updating these findings by considering recent efforts to reallocate authority. We also review how state legislation guiding procurement and construction continues to burden decisionmaking and how support offered to individual institutions by the main system office remains problematic. Finally, we examine how faculty labor relations set limits on some directions of possible change.

State System Governance Structure Sometimes Allows Political Concerns to Outweigh System Needs

The membership of the Board of Governors, which oversees the State System, includes the governor and several legislators. The state system and university officials reported in interviews that the inclusion of legislators, rooted in the State System's founding legislation (Act 188), and the political context in which the board operates have sometimes allowed political concerns to take precedence over the needs of the system and its universities.

While it is common for the boards of higher education systems to include ex-officio members with voting rights (e.g., state governor, lieutenant governor, legislators, and secretary of education), they vary in the extent to which legislators are included. In North Carolina, for example, the public higher education system has five legislators serving on its board. Other systems—such as New York, Ohio, Maryland, and Maine—do not include any legislators on their boards. But even if legislators are not actual board members, politics permeates the boards through other means, such as gubernatorial appointments and legislative confirmations of appointees to boards. Thus, the effectiveness of the boards is not solely influenced by legislator representation, but also by the extent to which the governance structure allows members to infuse their partisan views in education discussions.

Our interviews and findings from the 2017 NCHEMS report indicated that the Board of Governors overseeing the State System is influenced to a large extent by the ideologies and political interests of its members, hindering open discussions and making it difficult for a board to take stances or make decisions that benefit the system without being concerned about the political ramifications. During interviews with RAND staff, several institutions brought up the 2016 faculty strike to illustrate how the governance structure is influenced by political interests. The strike was the result of a breakdown in communication between the State System and the statewide faculty union regarding compensation, health insurance costs, and pay and working conditions for temporary faculty. In this specific event, according to the interviews, the Board of Governors supported the State System's stance on compensation, even knowing that it might lead to a strike. When the strike actually occurred, however, the board and the governor came under pressure from their constituencies that led them to exert pressure on the State System to settle the contract with the statewide faculty union despite the considerable financial implications that settlement had for the system.

Conflict Can Arise When Board Members Also Serve on the Council of Trustees

Another structural aspect rooted in Act 188 promotes conflicts of interest. This is because the Board of Governors members are allowed to serve simultaneously on individual State System institutions' COTs. Specifically, five board members are required to be trustees of constituent institutions. As defined by Act 188, COT members have assigned roles in reviewing and recommending presidential appointments; being involved in the retention and dismissal of the president; informing institutional policies and programs; and reviewing and approving fees and budget requirements. However, some of our interviewees questioned how COT members could serve without being affected by conflicts of interest. Individuals who serve on both the Board of Governors and a COT have dual roles that can conflict with each other, especially when the statewide interest represented by the board is not aligned with how COT members see the interests of their specific institutions (NCHEMS, 2017).

Another concern raised by our interviewees relates to the selection and appointment of the COT members. According to Act 188, trustees are nominated and appointed by the governor with advice and consent from the state senate. However, many institutions were critical of the selection process. Specifically, members of institutions said the selection of individuals is not based on transparent criteria or abilities. Some of the individuals selected do not have the appropriate skills to perform their roles and support the needs of individual universities. For example, COTs have fiduciary responsibilities to review and approve annual operating and capital budget recommendations made by the university president. Yet some COT members do not have the business background or training to review budgets and determine whether the president's recommendations are reasonable. COT members reported that some institutions limited members' review and input on institutional related issues because of lack of confidence in their abilities.

Governance Structure Is Bureaucratic and Does Not Promote Accountability

As defined by Act 188, the roles and responsibilities of the Board of Governors, CO, university presidents, and COTs overlap in some areas and are ambiguous in others (Commonwealth of Pennsylvania, 2016; NCHEMS, 2017). The lack of clarity regarding which entity has authority increases bureaucracy and weakens efforts to hold the institutions accountable. In our review of different higher education systems, we found that some have similar multilayered governance structures, but others tend to have fewer governance entities at the institutional level than State System universities. For example, public higher education systems in California and Maine do not have COTs or any other governing structure at the institutional level. University of Maine member institutions have campus-level Boards of Visitors that serve as advisers to the campus president.

The multiple layers of authority and overlapping areas of responsibility in the State System result in institutions having to go through multiple levels of approval on many educational issues, thus delaying efforts. For example, many institutions have sought to respond to dwindling student enrollment by restructuring their academic programs and proposing new programs that would allow them to compete in new markets, attract new types of students, and increase revenue. Our interviewees reported that the approval process for new programs requires consent from both the Board of Governors and the COT, which hinders timely responsiveness. One institution indicated that the review process for new programs takes a year or more. Institutions questioned the need for two different entities to have the same program approval responsibilities and indicated that the delay puts them at a disadvantage because other higher education providers can respond to changes in student demographics and offer new programs more quickly. The CO shares this view and has been engaged in efforts to streamline the process. In particular, the board has now delegated its approval authority to the CO.

Decisionmaking Is Hampered by Limited Chancellor Authority

While Act 188 defines many roles of responsibility in the State System, the legislation does not clearly define the decision authority held by the Board of Governors and the chancellor. Act 188 provides the board with authorization to determine how much authority to assign to the chancellor, but the level of authority provided is inadequate (NCHEMS, 2017). In short, the chancellor has limited power to address the challenges facing the system or to hold institutions accountable. A critical area where the chancellor does not have adequate power is in negotiating collective bargaining agreements; to a substantial extent, this power rests with the board. As previously noted, institutions have reported that the structure and membership of the board leaves it vulnerable to the influence of the statewide faculty union. According to our interviewees, the board exerts pressure on the chancellor to accept multiyear employment agreements disconnected from any dedicated revenue sources or commitment from the state to pay for the agreements. Further complicating matters, the institutions have limited autonomy to implement policies, such as setting their own student tuition or managing their costs in human resources effectively, to respond to the cost ramifications of the employment agreements. It is noteworthy that the State System has implemented pricing flexibility pilots for tuition and student fees since 2014. This resulted in policy changes in January 2017 that provide for greater university pricing flexibility.

Another illustration of the chancellor's limited authority relates to initiatives that the universities have taken since the late 1990s to modernize their aging student housing. Today, a number of these new residence halls sit empty or underfilled because student enrollments have declined so quickly. There is significant contention over how this situation came to pass. According to the CO, the board asked the chancellor to follow a process, in partnership with the university presidents, that required market demand analyses, residence hall construction plans, and financial plans that were subject to market discipline. Because universities used public-private partnerships to build the halls, decisions rested with the university presidents and local affiliate leadership. Interviewees we spoke with at universities thought that the CO did not vet and manage these decisions. Following this process, university presidents might have authorized more buildings than advised by the CO because the chancellor lacked the power to direct the decisions. Today, a number of the universities and their affiliated foundations are burdened by debt resulting from these decisions.

Interviewees from State System institutions also reported that the CO and the board have fallen short in holding institutions accountable for management of operations and finances. The board and the CO have also failed to take action against institutions that have consistently mismanaged operations and finances due to lack of leadership at the institutional level. Cheyney University is an example that came up repeatedly during the interviews. There were adequate warning signs for many years about Cheyney's management of its operations and finances that negatively affected every aspect of the institution, including its administrative processes, quality of academic programs, and culture. But the board and the CO neither held the institution accountable nor intervened in a timely manner to address the seriousness of the situation. In 2015, Cheyney was put on probation by the Middle States Commission of Higher Education, and it continues to be on probation. To preserve the oldest historically black college, the board recently adopted a process by which the university's more than $30 million in system loans may be forgiven. According to our interviewees, the money came out of the State System's cash balance, which comprises the cash balances of all 14 universities and the CO. To the extent that the reserve represents funding to cover institutional deficits, other institutions now face greater risk in covering any deficits they might have.

Interviewees indicated that, because of its limited authority, institutions view the CO as playing the role of a regulatory office with the primary objective of monitoring whether institutions' policies and processes comply with policies set by the Board of Governors. Institutional leaders reported that different parts of the CO ask for information, often to check compliance, and these different requests overlap in the items they request. Institutional leaders also reported that the system office does not use the information it receives to offer strategic advice to help universities improve their performance. Institutions indicated that the CO should provide strategic leadership, should be able politically to respond to internal and external constituencies, should have leadership with technical expertise to manage budgets and employees and hold universities accountable, and should be entrepreneurial enough to create a compelling vision for the future of the entire system and manage competition with other universities.

It is important to mention that there have been efforts by the interim chancellor and Board of Governors to redesign and improve the State System after the release of the 2017 NCHEMS report. These efforts focus on areas over which the CO has authority. Other areas of related governance or allocation of authority are not addressed in these efforts. Specifically, the goals of CO efforts are to improve student outcomes, enhance the efficiency and effectiveness of the entire institutional system, and ensure strategic changes that support the system's long-term success. The board identified three priorities on which it is working: (1) ensuring student success, (2) leveraging the strengths of each of the universities to advance the system and (3) transforming governance and leadership. The CO has put together several working groups tasked with defining and addressing ways to achieve these priorities. The CO also has started reviewing its policies, eliminating those that are redundant or ineffective and developing new ones where needed.

Cumbersome State Rules Reportedly Add Costs and Delays

Because the universities under the State System are state-owned, they must deal with state regulatory rules and oversight pertaining to procurement and construction that is much more stringent than those dealt with by state-related universities. Specifically, the threshold part of Act 188, the Administrative Code, the Commonwealth Attorneys Act, the Procurement Code, and the Separations Act add layers of bureaucracy and take away universities' independent freedom to execute contracts. According to interviewees, these rules and regulations add costs and slow down institutional efforts to purchase services and improve facilities. First, institutions must obtain approvals even on small projects from the University Counsel and the Office of the Attorney General. The cost threshold for requiring project approval is very low—approximately $20,000. Second, for building construction of more than $4,000, institutions must prepare separate specifications, solicit separate bids, and award separate contracts for general construction, plumbing, heating and ventilating, and electrical work. Third, facility projects funded with commonwealth capital funds must be managed by the Department of General Services, adding more layers of bureaucracy and delays. Many institutions reported General Services work costs more and is of lower quality. Fourth, some procurements require the use of the state-mandated best-value procurement approach, which considers factors other than price when selecting vendors and contractors. Interviews indicated this process adds cost without adding value. Institutions also must contract at prevailing wages, which further increases operational expenses.

System Office Support and Services Do Not Always Meet the Needs of Individual Institutions

A number of interviewees from individual State System institutions suggested that the main system office does not provide needed support. As indicated earlier in this chapter, the CO has limited authority and involvement in strategic planning. The system asks for a variety of information from institutions to ensure external compliance, but too little time is spent examining data to inform institutions about their performance and areas in need of improvement. The action plans that institutions were required to submit were viewed as being lengthy, time-consuming, and providing no foundation for strategic planning (NCHEMS, 2017). Furthermore, interviewees indicated that interactions between the system office and institutions are inadequate, contributing to a lack of understanding on a variety of issues that institutions face. This lack of understanding of the unique context of each institution could have contributed to the current situation in which some policies, such as tuition setting, are systemwide and overlook regional variation and institutional competitive positions. It is important to note, however, that the system office has been more involved with institutions in the past several months and more responsive to institutional needs. The system office has mainstreamed the program approval process and is allowing institutions greater flexibility in setting tuition.

According to our State System interviews, the system office is engaged in efforts for shared services and contracts in the areas of legal counsel, employee benefits, labor relations, construction support, financial management system, strategic sourcing, intranet/internet services, library resources, and learning management systems. A few interviewees raised the issue that the institutions are paying the State System for services they do not utilize. Other institutions reported that the State System did not offer back-office services or unified management systems to support them and reduce their costs.

A few institutions suggested that the State System should be offering additional consolidated contracts to support institutions and reduce financial burdens. For example, institutions that are in rural areas would benefit if the system had one vendor contract for specific services across the 14 universities because it is harder to secure good vendors in those areas.

There have been efforts by institutions to share services and contracts. For example, Bloomsburg and Mansfield universities are sharing human resources and payroll functions, while West Chester and Cheyney universities are sharing services in landscaping, human resources, facilities management, procurement, finance, and environmental safety.

Faculty Labor Relations Limit Flexibility

Interviewees from the State System and its institutions reported a stressed relationship with the statewide faculty union. Interviewees noted that factors contributing to this strained relationship include the contract provisions and their enactment, as well as the collective bargaining agreement negotiation process. Interviewees from within the system and from individual institutions raised concerns regarding the contract's restrictive language. Specific concerns include the following:

- **Salary scale for faculty**: The current scale is uniform, does not take disciplines into account, and does not allow for market-based adjustment.
- **Salary categories of non-faculty staff**: Librarians, athletic directors, coaches, department chairs, and counselors are included under faculty and have the same salary schedule as faculty.
- **Salary scale for adjunct faculty**: Adjuncts are paid at full prorated salary.
- **Online teaching requirements and pay**: Faculty cannot be required to teach online classes unless it is defined in their letter of appointment. Faculty are required to be paid an additional $25 per student enrolled in online classes.
- **Cross-departmental teaching**: Faculty cannot share time in another department without faculty approval from the recipient department.
- **Temporary appointments**: Tenured faculty cannot be granted an academic scholar visitor status at other State System institutions without approval from both the sending and receiving institutions.
- **Faculty seniority**: Institutions cannot retain highly rated faculty over more-senior faculty.
- **Faculty hiring**: Institutions cannot hire new faculty without the approval of all faculty in the department.
- **Part-time faculty hiring**: Institutions cannot hire part-time faculty to total time equal to more than 25 percent of FTE without faculty approval.

Institutional representatives interviewed in the course of this study view the restrictions listed here as costly and having a general negative impact on efforts to restructure academic programs and respond to current circumstances of inadequate state support funds and changes in student demographics. Interviewees also indicated that having faculty salary scales that are undifferentiated by field of study or locale of institution add costs and make it difficult to be competitive in hiring and retaining faculty from certain high-demand fields. Similarly, interviewees reported that salaries are high for nonfaculty staff, who are held to the same work schedule as faculty even though the natures of their jobs are different. For example, counselors sometimes have to provide student support during intersession or summer sessions—but in order for them to be available during those times, institutions would need to issue an additional contract. As another example, many institutions are moving toward developing online offerings and consolidating programs to be more competitive and efficient. Interviewees from these institutions reported that the faculty contract language limits their level of managerial autonomy and prerogative to move faculty around and reassign them to different programs, courses, and departments in response to restructuring and consolidation. In addition, the contract makes it

20

difficult to move faculty across State System institutions and realign the workforce with institutional needs. Interviewees also reported that the faculty contract makes it difficult to retrench or lay off staff because the union would challenge those decisions and file grievances.

State System Faculty Contracts May Be More Restrictive in Certain Areas Than Those Offered in Other Systems

We interviewed Pennsylvania union leaders, two academics who specialize in labor unions, and a local faculty union leader in California. We also reviewed faculty contracts for the states of New York, New Jersey, Maine, and California on four dimensions that State System universities consistently raised as critical issues: faculty compensation, online learning, adjunct faculty compensation, and retrenchment. Table B.13 in Appendix B compares contract language from these five states along these dimensions.

Our interviews and reviews of faculty contracts in the other four states suggest that the State System faculty contract is similar to others in terms of overall structure and areas addressed. The State System faculty contract differs in that it has more-restrictive and more-detailed language that limits managerial prerogative and latitude for negotiations than we found in the contracts for some of the other four states. For example, in Maine, New York, California, and New Jersey, colleges have more discretion in placing faculty on the salary schedule. In New York, the faculty contract offers stipends to compensate for cost of living, depending on geographical areas. Specifically, the high-cost New York metropolitan area has a 10-percent increase cost-of-living differential. In California, the contract allows college presidents to grant increases in salaries for certain faculty. The faculty contract in New Jersey offers several degrees of flexibility, including three defined salary ranges for each faculty rank (12 scales in all) and the ability for colleges to place new faculty on any step of any applicable range. In addition, colleges are allowed to set salaries within a very broad range for up to 5 percent of faculty, presumably to attract and retain notable faculty members.

Unlike Pennsylvania, faculty contracts in New Jersey and California do not require faculty approval to teach online classes. But the contracts do take workload considerations into account. The faculty contracts in Maine regarding distance learning are similar to the ones in Pennsylvania, where faculty can decline to teach online programs if such programs were not specified in the faculty letters of appointment.

While State System adjunct faculty are paid at the full prorated salary of a full-time faculty member, other states that we reviewed compensate adjunct faculty at a lower rate. In New Jersey, adjunct faculty receive about 60 percent of the prorated equivalent of the lowest possible assistant faculty salary. In California, adjunct faculty are prorated at the FTE of the lowest paid instructor level.

In terms of retrenchments, all faculty contracts in the four states and Pennsylvania implement the seniority system. In addition, most faculty contracts (including those of the State System) have leeway to allow the retention of faculty with necessary skills over more-senior faculty in areas that are very specialized and require special skills.

The way in which the State System faculty union contract is negotiated is another point of contention among the various entities. Institutions reported that these negotiations are politicized and occur without institutions' or the State System's input. Institutions indicated that the faculty contract is primarily negotiated at the state level and approved by the Board of Governors without regard for inadequate state appropriations or the fact that institutions cannot set their own tuition rates to offset the lack of state support. Institutions are left on their own to find other ways to manage the increased costs resulting from the salary rates set by the faculty contract. Institutions reported engaging in different efforts in response to increased faculty salaries while student enrollment declines. These efforts include reducing support staff, consolidating programs, shifting from flat rates to per-credit tuition (with Board of Governors approval), and retrenching faculty.

The enactment of collective bargaining agreements is also challenging to institutions. Without doubt, these negotiations have contributed to the mistrust between the institutions and the statewide faculty union. Institutions also reported that the local union representatives do not have much say—even when they do agree with the institutions, their decisions are overturned by the statewide union. For example, one institution indicated that it was able to reach an agreement with the local union representative to prorate a faculty member's salary during the summer based on student enrollment in his or her class. The faculty were committed to this change, but the statewide union disagreed, and the institution could not move forward with its proposal.

State System Universities Focus on Limited Markets

A further set of challenges arise from the limited markets that State System universities serve. They are focused largely on in-state undergraduate students and historically have enrolled large numbers of students pursuing degrees in education, consistent with their history as developing from teacher training colleges. They have also made very uneven use of distance education to serve working students and students outside their traditional service areas.

State System Universities Enroll Mostly In-State Undergraduate Students

State System universities' enrollment include a heavy concentration of undergraduate students. Table 3.1 shows the fraction of enrollment in each sector accounted for by graduate students. While graduate students account for 9.7 percent of State System enrollment, that number is 16.9 percent for state-related universities and 23.6 percent for four-year private colleges and universities. These percentages have been largely stable over the 2010–2016 period (not shown in the table). The state-related and four-year private institutions might thus have more options to expand their graduate programs as a way to stabilize enrollments when the number of traditional-age undergraduate students in the state declines.

22

The State System enrolls mostly in-state students, with just 12.4 percent of first-time undergraduates coming from out of state in 2016, as shown in Table 3.2. By contrast, state-related universities enrolled 33.4 percent from out of state, a fraction that has grown substantially in the past ten years. Private universities have long maintained slightly more than 50 percent of their undergraduate enrollments from out of state.

Table 3.1. Students by Level and Sector, 2016

Institution	Undergraduate	Graduate	Total	Graduate Percentage of Total
State System	84,755	9,093	93,848	9.7
State-related	131,567	26,752	158,319	16.9
Community colleges	70,924	0	70,924	0.0
Four-year private	167,825	51,736	219,562	23.6

SOURCE: National Center for Education Statistics, undated.
NOTE: All enrollments are Fall FTE.

Table 3.2. Percentage of First-Time Undergraduate Students from Outside Pennsylvania, 2006–2016

Institution	2006	2008	2010	2012	2014	2016
State System	11.8	11.9	13.1	12.9	11.6	12.4
State-related	23.4	24.1	26.2	28.1	30.1	33.4
Community colleges	2.2	1.7	1.9	1.6	1.6	2.0
Four-year private	51.2	51.7	53.1	53.5	54.1	53.5

SOURCE: National Center for Education Statistics, undated.
NOTE: Data collected every other year in IPEDS.

Enrollments Have Declined in Traditional State System Fields of Study and Increased in Some High-Demand Fields

State System universities historically educated teachers, and education accounted for a large fraction of enrollments. But education enrollments have declined throughout the state. The number of State System–awarded education degrees declined 34.1 percent between 2010 and 2016, as shown in Table 3.3. These declines are broadly in line with other sectors. The State System has added 66.5 percent in health degrees awarded, offsetting part of the decline in education, but it has added only 9 percent in engineering degrees awarded, while the state-related and four-year private institutions have added about 36 percent each. Appendix Table B.3 provides detailed trends summarized in Table 3.3.

Table 3.3. Change in Total Degrees Awarded by Broad Field and Sector, 2010–2016 (percentage)

Field	State System	State-Related	Community Colleges	Four-Year Private
Business	10.3	9.1	0.8	−0.9
Education	−34.1	−31.9	−37.6	−27.1
Engineering	9.0	36.5	16.8	36.0
Fine Arts	−9.7	−25.5	72.5	6.3
Health	66.5	27.5	4.9	35.2
Legal	−23.6	−21.2	−24.4	30.7
Liberal Arts	3.4	−8.1	20.3	−14.7
Science	21.0	32.2	53.2	30.4
Social Science	10.9	5.3	25.1	6.6

SOURCE: National Center for Education Statistics, undated.

Distance Education Varies Markedly Across State System Universities

Universities are increasingly reaching students, especially working students beyond traditional college age, through distance education. As a whole in 2016, the State System was teaching 8.7 percent of its total enrollment entirely by distance education (not including students taking a mix of distance and face-to-face courses), as shown in Table 3.4. This fraction is similar to the fractions in the state-related and four-year private sectors in Pennsylvania and represents notable growth over the five-year period for which these data are available (2012–2016).

Nonetheless, some State System universities have moved much more aggressively into offering distance education than others. As Table 3.5 shows, only four universities teach more than 10 percent of their enrollment entirely by distance education (California, Clarion, Edinboro, and Slippery Rock). Each of these four has significantly increased the fraction of its enrollment taught entirely by distance between 2012 and 2016.

While institutions could choose to use different approaches to deliver education, and thus show variation in use of distance learning, the relatively low usage rates at most State System universities are likely to inhibit the universities from reaching people already in the workforce as potential students. Thus, it could be that some structural or historical factors are inhibiting State System universities from developing distance learning (and other programs) that could support adult learning and workforce development. One factor that might have inhibited growth in 100-percent distance education is that such students were not eligible for state PHEAA grants. A recent law (Act 5 of 2018) made these students eligible, so universities might see more demand for 100-percent distance education from state residents.

Because State System universities are especially dependent on their local areas for enrollments, it seems unlikely that the majority of State System institutions will be able to adapt to stabilize their enrollments as these local populations decline, unless the institutions and system operate under significantly different approaches than they do now.

Table 3.4. Distance Education Students as a Percentage of Total Enrollment by Sector, 2012–2016

Institution	2012	2013	2014	2015	2016
State System	5.4	5.8	6.5	7.6	8.7
State-related	6.2	6.9	7.7	8.6	9.0
Community colleges	9.3	9.4	9.9	10.9	11.9
Four-year private	6.3	6.6	6.9	7.6	8.9

SOURCE: National Center for Education Statistics, undated.
NOTE: Students in 100-percent distance education; does not include students taking a mix of distance and face-to-face courses.

Table 3.5. Distance Education Students as a Percentage of Total Enrollment at State System Universities, 2012–2016

University	2012	2013	2014	2015	2016
Bloomsburg	0.9	0.9	1.0	1.8	1.7
California	23.9	26.0	28.8	33.3	36.3
Cheyney	0.0	0.2	0.2	0.6	0.0
Clarion	21.1	22.4	23.1	24.6	26.7
East Stroudsburg	0.3	0.9	1.1	1.4	2.2
Edinboro	10.6	11.1	12.2	15.1	16.9
Indiana	1.6	1.6	2.1	2.6	3.0
Kutztown	1.1	0.9	0.9	1.4	2.3
Lock Haven	5.5	6.4	6.7	7.7	7.7
Mansfield	11.1	12.2	10.9	9.7	8.3
Millersville	1.4	1.6	1.8	2.6	4.7
Shippensburg	0.9	0.9	2.1	2.1	2.2
Slippery Rock	6.6	7.6	9.9	11.6	12.7
West Chester	0.7	1.1	2.1	2.9	4.9

SOURCE: National Center for Education Statistics, undated.
NOTE: Students in 100-percent distance education. Does not include students taking a mix of distance and face-to-face courses.

Chapter Four

Consequences of Internal and External Challenges for State System Universities and Students

As discussed in the previous two chapters, the State System faces significant external and internal challenges to viable sustainability. This chapter presents a deeper look at the challenges by demonstrating how they intersect and can ultimately negatively affect State System institutions and their students. Particular attention is paid to enrollment figures and institutional financial health, student learning outcomes, costs, and available services. The findings here inform the five options described and discussed in the next chapter.

Consequences for Institutions

Enrollment Is Declining at Most State System Universities

Overall enrollments have declined 12.9 percent from 2010 to 2016 at State System universities, although the pattern differs markedly for each individual university, as shown in Figure 4.1. Only West Chester has increased its enrollment over this period, with an increase of 16 percent. Three universities have experienced declines of less than 10 percent: Slippery Rock, Bloomsburg, and East Stroudsburg. Four universities have experienced declines between 10 and 20 percent: Millersville, Indiana, Shippensburg, and Kutztown. Three universities have seen declines between 20 and 30 percent: Lock Haven, California, and Edinboro. Finally, three universities have seen declines of 30 percent or more: Clarion's enrollment has dropped 30 percent, Mansfield's enrollment has dropped 34 percent, and Cheyney's enrollment has dropped 52 percent.

Table 4.1 provides the enrollment figures in 2010 and 2016 that define these patterns.

Although Student Enrollment Has Declined at Most State System Universities, Staffing Has Not Changed in Proportion

While student enrollments have declined in the State System as a whole, staffing reductions have been much more modest. Table 4.2 shows the change in student FTE enrollment from 2010 to 2016 and the corresponding changes in instructional and noninstructional staff. State System enrollments have declined 12.9 percent, but instructional staff have been reduced only 2.3 percent and noninstructional staff 5.9 percent over the same period. Because staffing costs are the largest component of budgets in higher education, it is important for long-term financial health that institutions be able to grow enrollments to match staffing or shrink staffing to match enrollments.

Figure 4.1. Change in Student Enrollments (Fall FTE) at State System Universities, 2010–2016

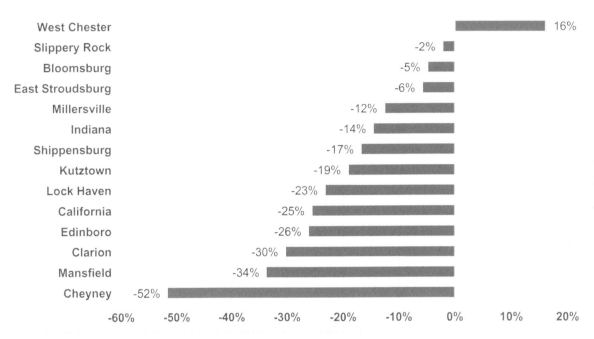

SOURCE: National Center for Education Statistics, undated.

Table 4.1. Student Enrollments (Fall FTE) at State System Universities, 2010–2016

| University | Students (Fall FTE) | | Change 2010–2016 |
	2010	2016	(%)
Bloomsburg	9,457	9,011	–4.7
California	8,372	6,242	–25.4
Cheyney	1,457	705	–51.6
Clarion	6,225	4,345	–30.2
East Stroudsburg	6,656	6,278	–5.7
Edinboro	7,351	5,436	–26.0
Indiana	13,738	11,753	–14.4
Kutztown	9,784	7,927	–19.0
Lock Haven	5,116	3,937	–23.0
Mansfield	3,054	2,027	–33.6
Millersville	7,796	6,826	–12.4
Shippensburg	7,564	6,303	–16.7
Slippery Rock	8,256	8,087	–2.1
West Chester	12,904	14,971	16.0

SOURCE: National Center for Education Statistics, undated.

Table 4.2. Students and Staff by Sector, 2010 and 2016

Institution	2010	2016	Change (%)
Students (Fall FTE)			
State System	107,730	93,848	−12.9
State-related	150,139	158,319	5.4
Community colleges	90,754	70,924	−21.9
Four-year private	223,457	219,562	−1.7
Instructional staff (FTE)			
State System	4,999	4,886	−2.3
State-related	12,989	13,953	7.4
Community colleges	4,861	4,593	−5.5
Four-year private	17,650	18,814	6.6
Noninstructional staff (FTE)			
State System	6,943	6,531	−5.9
State-related	27,510	27,562	0.2
Community colleges	4,740	4,590	−3.2
Four-year private	41,981	44,796	6.7

SOURCE: National Center for Education Statistics, undated.

The state-related and four-year private sectors have had much more stable enrollments. The state-related sector has grown enrollments by 5.4 percent over this period and grown instructional staff, although not noninstructional staff. The four-year private sector has lost 1.7 percent in enrollment but actually added both instructional and noninstructional staff, which suggests that this sector also might be experiencing financial strain.[1]

These patterns have played out differently at the different State System universities. As shown in Figure 4.1 and in Table 4.3, only one university, West Chester, gained student enrollment between 2010 and 2016. Seven universities lost up to 20 percent of their 2010 enrollment, and six lost more than 20 percent. Appendix Table B.8 contains a more complete version of Table 4.3.

All but one of the 13 universities that lost enrollment have been able to reduce either instructional or noninstructional staff, and generally both categories. At almost all of these universities, however, they have not reduced staff as quickly as student enrollments have declined. Indeed, one university with a moderate enrollment decline (Bloomsburg) even added

---

[1] While we focus on the period from 2010 to 2016, there was significant growth in all sectors between 2006 and 2010. Viewed over the ten-year period from 2006 to 2016, the State System's enrollment declined by 4.2 percent, state-related universities' enrollment increased by 14.4 percent, community college enrollment increased by 1.8 percent, and four-year private institutions' enrollment increased by 6.8 percent. Even measured over this somewhat more favorable ten-year period, the State System's enrollment declined while the other three sectors enrollment increased.

Table 4.3. Change in Students and Staffing at State System Universities, 2010–2016

University	Change 2010–2016 (%)		
	Students	Instructional Staff	Noninstructional Staff
Bloomsburg	−4.7	2.6	5.2
California	−25.4	0.3	−20.6
Cheyney	−51.6	−33.5	−44.1
Clarion	−30.2	−20.9	−4.5
East Stroudsburg	−5.7	−6.3	−14.7
Edinboro	−26.0	−18.1	−7.8
Indiana	−14.4	−1.3	−3.0
Kutztown	−19.0	−4.4	−7.2
Lock Haven	−23.0	−9.5	−9.7
Mansfield	−33.6	−12.9	−14.8
Millersville	−12.4	5.3	−5.2
Shippensburg	−16.7	−11.8	−4.7
Slippery Rock	−2.1	−1.6	−3.0
West Chester	16.0	24.6	10.3

SOURCE: National Center for Education Statistics, undated.

some staff as student enrollments declined. It can be difficult to reduce staffing proportionally to declining enrollments because certain functions have to be maintained even as enrollment declines. Nonetheless, long-term viability demands that universities be able to adjust their staffing to match enrollment and, hence, funding levels. These staffing adjustments should address both the number of staff and the assignment of staff to functions that support the mission and health of the institution.

Some State System Universities Are Experiencing Significant Financial Stress and Others Are Heading in That Direction

When we examine indicators of financial health, we see that some State System universities are showing signs of stress and others are heading in a troubling direction. These findings are likely closely related to the findings in the previous sections—specifically, that enrollments have been declining and staffing has not been reduced in proportion.

We specifically examine four indicators of financial health, based on the practices that the Moody's bond rating agency uses to assess the creditworthiness of public higher education institutions (Moody's, 2017). We focus most on annual surpluses or deficits as a measure of whether universities have sufficient revenue to fund their annual operations. In accounting terms, these surpluses or deficits are known as *change in net position*. Because there is a fair amount of annual volatility in many of the financial measures, we take a moving three-year average of all financial figures, and exclude all one-time adjustments to net position. Figure 4.2 graphs the three-year average of surpluses or deficits. Each cluster of bars represents the 14 State System universities for one three-year period (ending in the year marked). In the early years, most universities show surpluses. During the Great Recession, a few universities show deficits in each period, but most remain in surplus. In the most recent three years, however, the pattern changes significantly. More universities are experiencing deficits over time and fewer surpluses.

Figure 4.2. Change in Net Position (Surplus or Deficit), Three-Year Average at State System Universities, 2006–2008 to 2014–2016

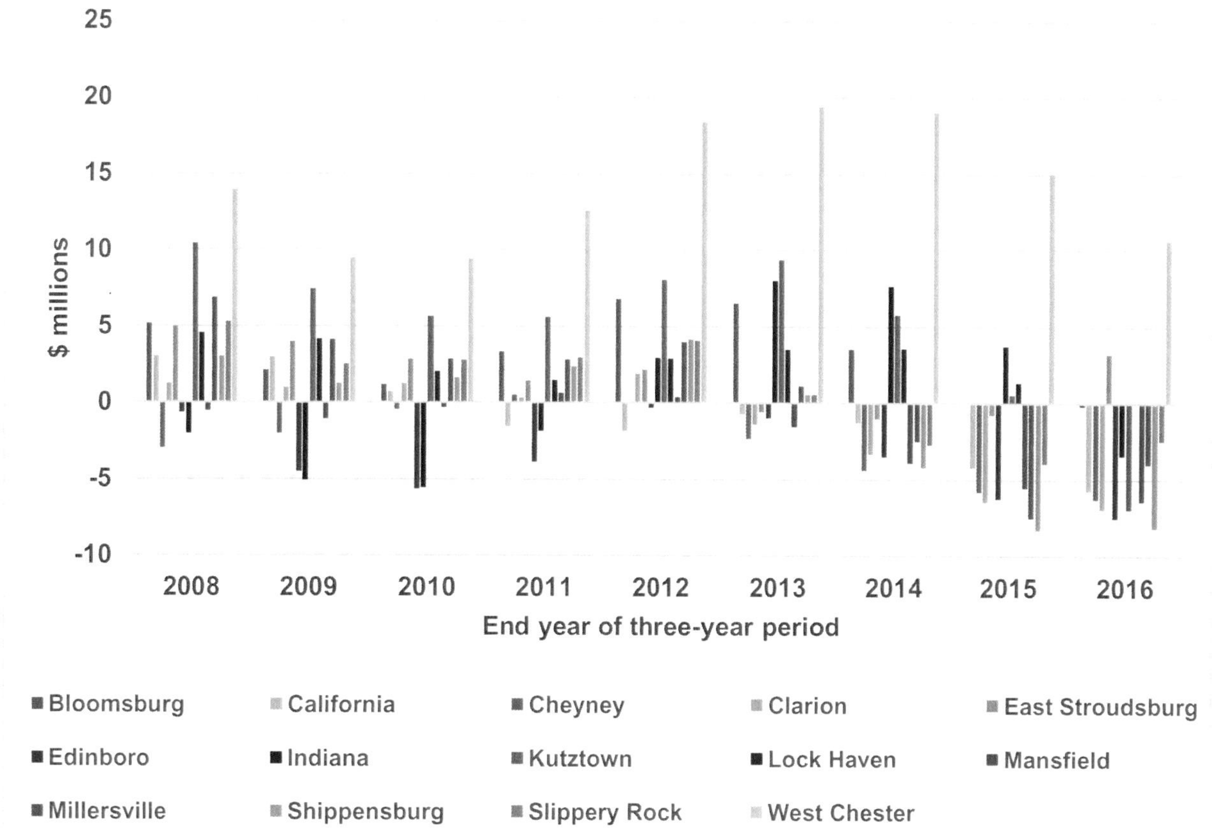

SOURCE: National Center for Education Statistics, undated.
NOTE: Each bar represents one of the 14 State System universities, shown in alphabetical order. All adjustments to net position, such as one-time changes in liabilities, are excluded.

The last two years shown in Figure 4.2 are partly affected by 2015 changes in governmental accounting standards that require public universities to record long-term liabilities for retiree pension benefits. But the pattern up to 2014 and the smoothing that results from three-year averages indicate that concern about deficits is warranted, despite the effects of this accounting change.

Figures B.2–B.4 and Tables B.9–B.12 in Appendix B present the detailed results of the other three financial indicators we examined, and the appendix text provides some notes and explanations of the indicators: approximated cash flow, the ratio of cash flow to long-term debt, and the ratio of long-term debt to total revenue. All three of the other indicators are generally worsening over time, although they display more variation across universities than the surpluses and deficits shown in Figure 4.2. Cash flow is decreasing and long-term debt is increasing, compared with institutional ability to generate funds to repay that debt.

These other indicators provide important context. While change in net position has turned negative for most universities, as shown in Figure 4.2, approximated cash flow is more positive: Ten universities are positive on this measure in 2016, one is very slightly negative, and three are somewhat more negative. These findings indicate that, despite the trend in Figure 4.2, most State System universities still have the ability to fund their operations. But the overall negative trends, including reduction in cash flow levels, indicate that more universities will experience financial stress in the future if conditions do not change.

The variation in financial indicators across universities is consistent with variation in enrollment and staffing trends. Overall trends are negative, but some universities are managing considerably better than others because they either face less challenging circumstances or they have been able to manage challenges better than their peers. For instance, West Chester is located in the Philadelphia area with a large and growing population. West Chester is the only university to grow enrollment between 2010 and 2016, contributing to relatively healthy finances with significant operating surpluses. Bloomsburg also draws heavily from the Philadelphia area. While Bloomsburg's enrollment has declined about 5 percent over this period and its operating surpluses have declined to near zero, it is doing better than most of the other State System universities, which are experiencing greater declines in enrollment and operating deficits. Slippery Rock has faced demographic challenges in its region but has been able to maintain nearly steady enrollment over this period, perhaps because it has substantially increased distance learning and added degree programs to attract student interest.

Consequences for Students

Costs Have Been Increasing and Could Increase Further

The State System has traditionally been an affordable option for Pennsylvania students to pursue a bachelor's degree. Over the past decade, tuition, fees, and room and board have risen at both State System and at competing institutions. Figure 4.3 shows the trend in tuition and required fees for in-state students. State System tuition levels remain more affordable than state-related institutions—either their main campuses or their branch campuses, which have different tuition and fees.

Room and board charges, shown in Figure 4.4, are increasing even faster. Over the period from 2007 to 2016, State System room and board charges rose much faster than at competing institutions, reaching a level equal to the state-related institutions.

Tables B.4 and B.5 in Appendix B provide additional data on tuition, fees, and room and board.

While the trend in tuition has been comparable to other publicly supported alternatives over the past decade, this trend could worsen in the future. Because the pressure on enrollments and finances at State System universities seems to be greater than at the state-related universities, State System universities might have to increase tuition and fees faster than the state-related universities.

Figure 4.3. Median Tuition and Mandatory Fees for In-State Students, by Sector, 2007–2016

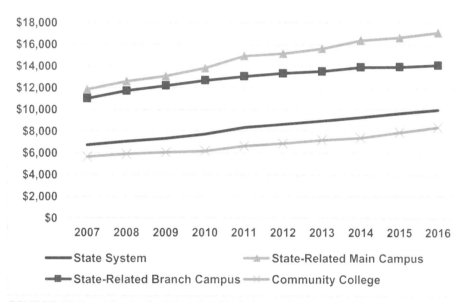

SOURCE: National Center for Education Statistics, undated.

32

Figure 4.4. Median On-Campus Room and Board, by Sector, 2007–2016

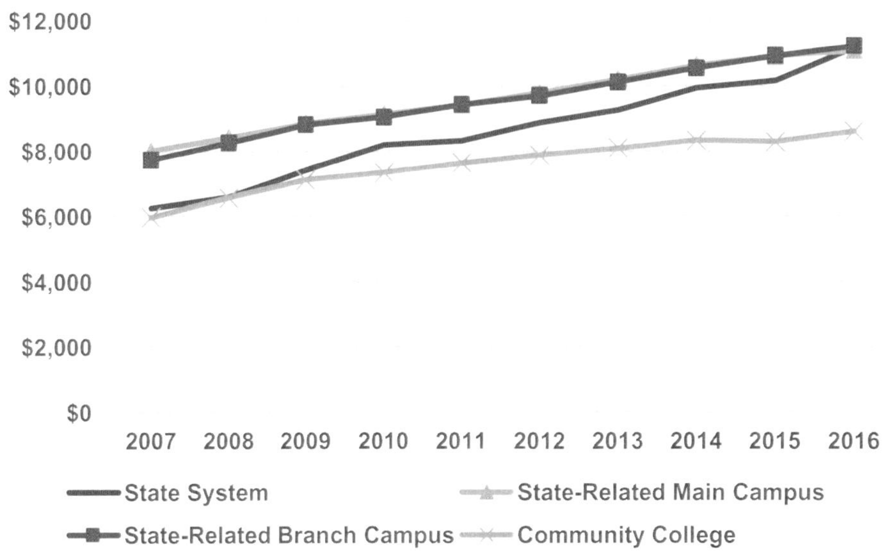

SOURCE: National Center for Education Statistics, undated.

Student Services Have Been Reduced

Some students and staff from student services reported that inadequate state funding and revenue from tuition have affected the support provided to students. Interviewees indicated that such services were the first to be downscaled. It also increased competition for available funds among support service offices. Support staff were either let go or had to adjust their work hours. Support staff also started borrowing office materials and supplies from other departments and had to cut down on promotional material designed to attract more students. Some reported that efforts that are essential for student success, such as counseling and student retention initiatives, have also been curtailed.

Student Outcomes Show Variation

Figure 4.5 shows that graduation rates at State System universities average 56.6 percent in six years, slightly above the national average of 54.7 percent for four-year public colleges and universities in 2016.[2] Graduation rates at Pennsylvania state-related and four-year private institutions are more notably above the national averages and the State System. These differences could reflect a different mix of students and their needs—and, possibly, better academic and student services offered at state-related and private institutions.

---

[2] This rate counts students who graduate from the same State System university where they start, which is the standard method. The CO has calculated that counting graduation from any State System university increases the overall six-year State System graduation rate by five percentage points in 2016.

As Table B.6 in Appendix B shows, the graduation rates at all sectors have been increasing, both in absolute terms and compared with the national averages between 2006 and 2016. These increases are most significant for the state-related universities.

Figure 4.5. Six-Year Graduation Rates by Sector, with National Averages, 2016

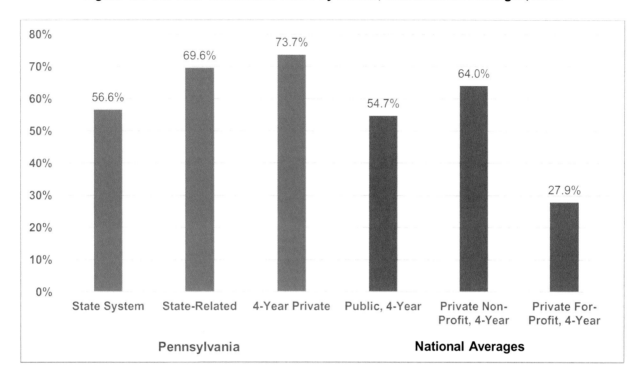

SOURCE: National Center for Education Statistics, undated. National averages from IPEDS Trend Generator.
NOTE: Rates measure the percentage of first-time bachelor's-seeking students who graduate within the specified period from the same institution.

There is variation across the State System universities. West Chester, Slippery Rock, Bloomsburg, and Millersville have the highest rates, with six-year graduation rates ranging from 61 percent to 70 percent in 2016. Cheyney is a notable outlier, with just 16 percent graduating within six years. The other universities generally have six-year rates around 50 percent, as illustrated in Figure 4.6. Table B.7 in Appendix B shows that changes across universities have been mixed. Seven of the 14 universities have shown an increase in the six-year graduation rate between 2006 and 2016. The others have shown level or declining graduation rates.

Figure 4.6. Six-Year Graduation Rates at State System Universities, 2016

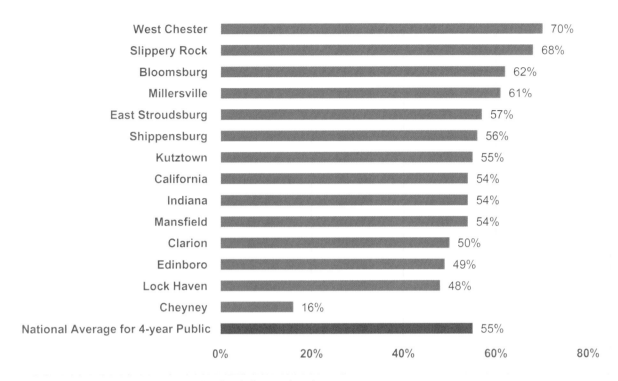

SOURCE: National Center for Education Statistics, undated.
NOTE: Rates measure the percentage of first-time bachelor's-seeking students who graduate within the specified period from the same institution.

Chapter Five

Options to Address Challenges

As the previous chapters suggest, State System universities face declining demographics in their traditional age and service regions, limited state funding, and competition from a large number of alternative higher education providers in Pennsylvania. Moreover, the current State System governance structures are political and bureaucratic, and they have failed to address important signs of serious institutional difficulties in the past. State rules limit flexibility and increase costs. The central system office's supports and services are not valued by all the universities. Faculty labor relations limit the universities' ability to respond to changing markets by restructuring programs or shrinking staff size to match demand.

These challenges have had an immediate effect. Several State System universities are in financial difficulty. Others are likely to join them if corrective actions are not taken to increase flexibility and responsiveness to external changes. Students are likely to be affected as well; learning outcomes and services could be limited while tuition bills rise.

To help the state address these challenges, we developed and assessed five options for change based on the inputs of various stakeholders, review of experiences in other states, and the research team's own ideas. In this chapter, we present the objectives used to guide the evaluation of options; a description of broad strategies needed for systemic change; and five options and implementation requirements, along with a description of how a combination of options might play out. We close with a brief examination of the state's university governance challenge.

Objectives Guided the Development of Options

Based on our analysis of the current situation and goals expressed in stakeholder interviews, we developed six objectives to guide the development of options:

1. Strengthen financially weak institutions.
2. Adjust the size of campus facilities and staffing to match enrollments.
3. Restructure programs for greater efficiency and responsiveness to enrollment trends.
4. Maintain access to college education for Pennsylvanians at an affordable price.
5. Preserve the historic mission and identity of current universities.
6. Avoid difficult implementation requirements.

It is probably not feasible to meet all six objectives fully, but the objectives serve as a useful way to compare the options we developed and highlight the trade-offs that the various options entail.

Broad Strategies for Change

Promising strategies include giving greater autonomy to universities that have demonstrated capacity to manage while also providing support and pathways that allow struggling institutions to become healthier. In addition, universities need greater flexibility in managing their workforces to adapt to changes.

Some strategies could involve university mergers. Closures are not recommended because they are usually very difficult politically and practically. Apart from the political pressure that student and employee groups might exert to keep universities open, many of the State System universities are among the largest employers in their regions.

Several interviewees cited the example of Pitt's Titusville branch campus, which has experienced declining enrollments for years. Since 2010, enrollment has declined 45 percent, down to just 300 students. University officials cited "demographic forces impacting higher education institutions across the Commonwealth of Pennsylvania. The rural areas have been hit particularly hard. There's been a shift in the population of traditional college attendees" (Faust, 2018). Despite the decline in enrollments and the cost of operating the branch campus, Pitt decided after a long deliberation to keep the campus as a teaching and learning center, offering its space to other tenants who can offer programs at the site while continuing to offer some Pitt programs (Faust, 2018). Our interviewees cited this as an example of the difficulty of entirely closing even a branch campus at a state-related institution.

Long-term considerations of adjusting size and reallocating programs argue that the current State System division into 14 independent universities is a poor design for a challenging future, especially with the limited options to combine programs across universities. Instead of strategies that entail complete closure of current institutions, we favor attempts to maintain some academic programs at all or almost all of the current State System universities through some type of consolidation among institutions inside or outside the current system.

Other states wrestling with similar demographic changes have conducted mergers to make larger and stronger universities. Georgia (Gardner, 2017) and Maine (Gardner, 2018) have both undertaken these consolidations.

There is evidence that mergers could save costs through sharing overhead costs and back-office services and reducing administrative costs. In the short term, Georgia institutions have saved modest amounts of money in their consolidations, typically less than 1 percent of their annual operating budget as a result of streamlined administration (Gardner, 2017). In addition, a larger institution offers a greater scope to consolidate staff and functions across formerly separate institutions, which could take more time to realize. There is also evidence that mergers could improve access to quality programs and services and retention and graduation rates. Most of the consolidated Georgia institutions have increased retention rates substantially, although this may be due to simultaneous systemwide initiatives to boost retention. While it is too early to see the impact on graduation rates, the retention increases are a positive sign (Gardner, 2017). Maine universities have also increased retention rates and introduced new competency-based education approaches as a result of their mergers (Gardner, 2018).

Still, mergers are difficult to manage. They have sometimes led to increased tuition: A recent study (Quinton, 2017) found that the average merger of public universities led to a 7-percent increase in tuition, and that while mergers generally target reductions in costs, they sometimes fail to achieve cost savings. Finally, mergers can generate contention as functions combine. While Georgia did consolidate academic programs across merged universities, the process often generated friction among faculty that had to reconcile different curricula, teaching approaches, and academic cultures (Gardner, 2017).

Options for Change

Five major options have the potential to address the challenges that the universities in the State System are facing. It is also possible that the State System could adopt a combination of these options. Each of these options includes an entity, such as a system office or a central office, overseeing institutions. There are advantages to having such entities in place, if structured well. They could play an important role in coordinating programs and supports, set strategies, and facilitate leadership to ensure student success across institutions or campuses. Such entities are also critical for monitoring and holding State System universities or merged universities accountable. Otherwise, there is no incentive for institutions—especially fiscally weak institutions—to improve. We do not recommend each State System university becoming independent; this option would expect institutions to fend for themselves, thus creating conditions under which fiscally weak institutions could fail.

All potential choices for future action are described here.

Option 1: Keep Broad State System Structure, Including Current Individual Universities, but with Improvements

Under this option, the state system's overall governance structure, State System functions, and individual institutions' missions are preserved, though somewhat altered. This option upgrades the existing system to a certain extent by modifying the governance structure to reallocate authority so it is more balanced across the various system levels, and by freeing institutions from some state requirements, such as those for procurement and construction.

The NCHEMS report provides extensive detail on the changes needed under this option (NCHEMS, 2017). Here, we highlight the core restructuring aspects described by NCHEMS and delineate any deviation from their report.

- **Modify the Board of Governors membership to reduce political influence and conflicts of interest in the decisionmaking process of the State System**. This could be accomplished by changing the composition of the board so that it is better equipped to represent the interests and needs of the commonwealth and its diverse regions. That is, the board should include members that are less driven by partisan ideologies or political interests. One way of accomplishing this is having board members, except for the governor, who are lay citizens, rather than elected or appointed officials. A set of criteria for appointments should be established that emphasizes the sort of knowledge—including financial and legal expertise and educational leadership—that can be beneficial in effectively overseeing the State System.

- **Eliminate the COTs.** The current role played by these councils in the governance structure adds another layer of bureaucracy because they are tasked with reviewing and approving institutional policies, programs, and budgets. Our recommendation for elimination departs from the specifics of NCHEMS's recommendations.

- **Institutions, upon their own discretion, could establish an advisory board instead of the COT.** Following on the previous recommendation, the advisory board would offer support to the institution's administrators and faculty, provide input from key stakeholders regarding strategic direction, guide quality and program improvement, and assess program relevancy in relation to the labor market. Institutions would be responsible for determining the criteria (based on their needs) used to select the advisory members and for making the appointments. The advisory board would have no authority to evaluate presidents of the institutions. Such evaluations would be the responsibility of the CO.

- **Enhance the authority of the chancellor and provide more leeway to respond to challenges**. The chancellor should have a more significant leadership role in setting the vision of the State System and its universities, evaluating the performance of presidents and institutions and holding them accountable, providing support to struggling universities, providing recommendations to the board regarding institutional budget, and requiring institutions to share services.

- **Adopt a graduated autonomy approach for the presidents of institutions.** Institutions that demonstrate healthy enrollment and finances should be granted greater autonomy to manage their own resources and budgets with lighter oversight from the chancellor; institutions that are struggling with these aspects should be subject to greater oversight.

- **Provide institutions with more independence and freedom in how they conduct their contracts and procurement.** Relieve the institutions from the contractual and procurement constraints they have because of being state-owned.

Although these provisions do not change the faculty labor agreements in any direct way, a less political board and clearer authorities for the board and the chancellor could lead to an improved relationship between the faculty union and the State System, in which the union and system negotiate contracts that provide greater flexibility in managing the faculty workforce.

To accomplish these objectives, the option requires various sections of Act 188 to be amended through legislative actions. This includes modifying: (1) section 20–2004-A, which specifies the selection of the board; (2) sections 20–2008-A and 20–2009-A, which address the membership selection, roles, and functions of COTs; (3) sections 20–2005-A and 20–2010-A, which address the authority of the chancellor and of institution presidents; and (4) section 20–2003-A.1, which addresses the construction code and the procurement code.

Option 2: Keep Broad State System Structure with Improvements Accompanied by Regional Mergers of Universities

Option 2 preserves the state system's overall governance structure and State System functions but consolidates the current 14 universities into a smaller number, perhaps ranging from five to eight. As with Option 1, the system will be upgraded by modifying the current governance structure and reallocating authority so it is more balanced across the various system levels, and by relieving institutions from state procurement and construction requirements. However, under this option, weaker State System institutions within each region will be merged with those that are fiscally viable. It could be that a few institutions are not merged because they have good enrollment and financial prospects on their own.

The advantage of this option is that it could create economies of scale. If done well, it could provide more flexibility for institutions to reassign and move faculty across campuses to address declining student enrollment and limited state support. It could also allow sharing of administrative costs across locations. A key disadvantage is that the more financially healthy institutions could be negatively affected in terms of management, academic standing, and credit rating for debt issuance. On the other side, the weaker institutions that are merged are likely to see alterations in their historic missions and programs offered.

There are implementation issues that need to be considered in addition to modifying Act 188 through legislative action (as indicated in Option 1).

- **Understand the short-term costs of mergers**. The state and the State System should determine the short-term costs and benefits of such mergers. It could be that mergers are costly in the short term but might save the system significant amounts of money in the long run. Since 2010, there have been more than 40 mergers across nine states, with mixed results regarding cost savings.
- **Address debt**. If the merger approach is adopted, the State System or the state might need to assist the fiscally viable institution with taking on the debt incurred by fiscally weak institutions.
- **Modify labor agreements**. The State System and the faculty union will have to restructure contract terms to accommodate the combination of faculty across merged institutions. In particular, the contract will need to combine employee seniority lists across the formerly separate universities. The State System will have to work with the unions on the necessary modifications.

- **Establish committees across merged institutions**. There should be a committee representing the merged institutions that works collaboratively with the chancellor to help the merged institution thrive by identifying new opportunities for faculty and students and by determining which programs should continue, whether new programs should be put in place, and the basis on which faculty and staff members should be retained or let go. Discussions should also include (1) how to reduce administrative and bureaucratic costs, without reducing the quality of services to the students; (2) how to govern faculty across institutions; (3) what type of delivery methods should be considered, particularly in the context of the merged set of faculty expertise; (4) what degrees should be offered moving forward; (5) the name that a merged entity should carry; and (6) what other types of synergies might present themselves through a merger.
- **Coordinate mergers with accreditation agencies**. Mergers will require endorsement from accreditors to extend the universities' separate accreditations to accreditation for the combined entity.

Option 3: Merge State System Universities and Convert to State-Related Status

Under this option, the State System structure is eliminated and universities are converted to state-related status, following the principles currently applied to state-related universities. We do not advise granting independence to universities that are struggling or facing significant market challenges in the coming years. This option could be applied only to the stronger universities or to weaker universities that could be merged (e.g., regionally) with stronger ones prior to independence. The advantages and disadvantages discussed in Option 2 also apply to this option. The main difference is that this option releases the institutions from the constraints of Act 188. In addition, as discussed later in the section titled "Evaluating the Prospects for the Options," this option would likely jeopardize the current State System universities' valuable sovereign immunity from lawsuits, unless a special arrangement can be made to preserve immunity.

The state could choose to negotiate with each new state-related institution in the same manner that it does with the current four state-related universities. However, this option could result in five to eight new state-related universities, meaning that the state would have to negotiate with nine to 12 universities. The state might instead choose to create a higher education coordinating board that would adopt a formula for allocating state funding to state-related institutions.

To implement this option, several of the implementation steps of Option 2 are required: The debt the institutions have accrued needs to be addressed by the state, and labor agreements will require revision to reflect the merged institutions. Merged institutions need to establish committees to address which programs to continue and staff to retain, and mergers also need to be coordinated with accreditation agencies.

In addition, systemic changes are also required.

41

- **Repeal Act 188**. This step will need to be taken so that the institutions are released from their state-owned designation.
- **Create legal bindings**. Mergers should be enacted into law and the merged universities established as state-related institutions.
- **Establish legislation if a state coordinating board is selected**. Provide specific authorities for the coordinating board in law to enable it to carry out its assigned missions.
- **Consider bonds**. The merged universities can take on the primary obligation for repaying bonds issued by the former universities (perhaps with some state assistance in some cases), but the state might have to offer a guarantee for bonds in the event of default by the new universities because the State System is being eliminated.

Option 4: Place the State System Under the Management of a State-Related University

Rather than try to improve current governance arrangements or replace them with new ones, this option builds on the strong performance of the state-related universities. Unlike State System universities, which are mostly showing operating deficits, the large state-related universities—Penn State and Pitt —show substantial financial surpluses, particularly when the increases in their endowments are included. In addition, these universities are experiencing growing enrollment, perhaps as a result of their greater diversity in graduate and out-of-state enrollments and their strong reputations and rankings.

Under this option, the State System and all its institutions become managed by a large state-related university, presumably either Penn State or Pitt. This option preserves all institutions as they currently stand, along with their missions. The State System institutions continue to receive state support, based on the current procedure. Labor union relations and faculty contracts also continue as they are. The state-related parent university determines which functions should remain in the State System Office and which others are provided by sharing services. Each State System university will continue to be accredited separately.

The main change would be in governance and operations. The state-related university will have full control over the State System in the selection and appointment of Board of Governors members. The board will be accountable to the governing body of the state-related university. The state-related university will oversee personnel, business functions, and procurement. It could provide a shared service model for business operations and functions and for back-office and information-technology services. This administrative flexibility is designed to save costs at the State System institutions. The goal is to maximize the opportunities to strengthen the financial standing of the State System universities while keeping the institutions and their mission as intact as possible. State-related universities charge higher tuition and fees than State System universities, so it is possible that State System control by a state-related university could lead to tuition and fee increases, potentially worsening affordability for Pennsylvania families if institutional financial aid is not also increased. This option raises questions about whether the current State System universities' sovereign immunity from lawsuits would continue, as discussed later in the section titled "Evaluating the Prospects for the Options."

There are several implementation issues to be considered.

- **Evaluate risk level**. The state-related university would need a due diligence period to more deeply assess debt levels, finances, and levels of risk before adopting this option.
- **Modify Act 188 pertaining to the governance structure**. Board selection and assignment and contract and procurement regulations need to be modified through legislation (see Option 1 for the list of Act 188 amendments).
- **Ensure state funding commitment**. There needs to be commitment from the state regarding continued financial support to State System universities. This arrangement should include a dissolution option in the event that state support does not continue at least at previous levels.
- **Put in place short-term and long-term plans regarding this arrangement**. The state-related institution should assume this role for a defined period, after which it and the state should assess the universities' prospects and decide whether to continue this arrangement or transition to something else—for example, one of the other options presented here. The state should be ready to intervene and support the institutions if the arrangement is not to be continued.

Option 5: Merge State System Universities into State-Related Universities

Rather than try to improve current governance arrangements or replace them with new arrangements, a final option is to build on the strong performance of the state-related universities by merging State System universities into one or more of the state-related universities. Penn State or Pitt could provide a structure for current State System universities as branch campuses in their systems. In addition, as discussed later under "Illustrating Potential Merger Options," other state-related universities might also play a helpful role.

This option would likely result in the reduction of the current mission at some or all of the current State System universities as they are merged into the state-related system or systems. It seems likely that tuition and fee rates at the State System campuses would rise to levels similar to the state-related branch campuses, potentially worsening affordability for Pennsylvania families if institutional financial aid is not also increased. Under this option, the current universities' sovereign immunity would be lost, as discussed later in the section titled "Evaluating the Prospects for the Options."

As with other options, merged institutions need to establish committees to address how the academic programs could be integrated, whether institutional missions could be retained, how staff could be deployed or retained and whether State System campuses could maintain their degree-granting status.

In addition, key implementation steps are required.

- **Repeal Act 188 if no universities will remain in the State System.**
- **Plan a transition path for employee labor relations**. State-related universities do not have collective bargaining for most employees, so the merged institutions will require a transition plan for integrating employees with or without collective bargaining.
- **Coordinate institutional mergers with accreditors**.
- **Enact institutional mergers in law**. This option would require that all assets be given to the state-related parent institution, which would also accept all liabilities.
- **Consider bonds.** Because the State System is being eliminated, the state might have to offer a guarantee for bonds in the event of default by the state-related universities (though we consider default to be unlikely).

Using a Combination of Options

It is not necessary to treat all 14 State System universities the same or apply the same option to them all. Two (or perhaps more) of these options can be used in combination. For instance, a set of weaker universities can be merged into state-related universities as branch campuses (Option 5) while stronger universities or mergers are given independence (Option 3).

Illustrating Potential Merger Options

Open discussion of the future arrangements for State System universities entails some risk that students might be further discouraged from applying to some or all State System universities. As a result, we recommend that the General Assembly move as quickly as possible to select a preferred approach and begin implementation. For the same reason, we are not presenting specific combinations of institutional mergers that cover all 14 State System universities or details of how current State System universities could be assigned to state-related institutions under Option 5.

A number of the State System universities face significant challenges and should be considered as candidates for mergers. To illustrate the considerations involved in potential merger strategies, we discuss specific options for two of the State System universities that are facing especially severe challenges: Cheyney and Mansfield. Both have experienced enrollment declines of more than 30 percent since 2010. Cheyney has been running significant deficits and accumulating debt for most of the past decade. Mansfield has not experienced the same degree of financial stress yet, but its indicators are pointing in a similar direction.

As noted in the earlier section on "Broad Strategies for Change," we do not recommend that either university be closed. Options 1 and 4 provide approaches to continue operating both of these as distinct universities. Under Options 2, 3, and 5, we recommend that both of these institutions, as well as other universities that face significant challenges, be merged with stronger institutions to continue offering services at their current locations, perhaps with a reduced mission or scale.

Our first example, Cheyney, is the nation's oldest historically black college and one of two in the state. Because of its history and special mission, discussions of major changes are bound to be sensitive. The state may choose to provide an increased level of support that recognizes Cheyney's special mission and enables it, with sound management and oversight, to become healthy as an independent university that can continue its historical legacy and contemporary mission. If that support commitment is not forthcoming, we see several merger possibilities for Cheyney, each of which could preserve significant aspects of Cheyney's mission. The option that seems to have the greatest prospects of retaining Cheyney's historic mission is a merger with Lincoln University, a state-related historically black university located about 25 miles away (under Option 5). Cheyney and Lincoln could combine their programs and faculty to support their joint history and mission of access for African Americans and, by extension, other racial or ethnic minorities.

We see at least two other merger options. Cheyney could be merged with a stronger State System university in the same general region of the state, likely West Chester, with which it has already started to share support services (under Option 2 or 3). Or, it could be merged into Penn State as a regional campus (under Option 5). Because the parent institution under either of these two options does not share Cheyney's specific historical legacy and mission, it would be desirable to retain significant aspects of Cheyney's special mission to reach African Americans and other racial or ethnic minorities through continuing structures and programs, as well as offering students access to a broader set of academic programs from the parent institution.

Under any of these three merger options, Cheyney could focus on a more specific set of missions and programs, such as offering the first two years of undergraduate education with transfer to the parent institution for degree completion in some or all fields.

Our second example, Mansfield, is located in the state's far north, a region with few nearby alternatives for higher education. Declining regional population (and, perhaps, competition from the free tuition policy in nearby New York) has resulted in significant enrollment declines. It could be merged with a stronger State System university in the same general region of the state, likely Bloomsburg, with which it is already sharing some services (under Option 2 or 3). It could be merged into Penn State as a regional campus (under Option 5), which might be an attractive option to both parties because Penn State currently has no campus in this region. As described for Cheyney, either of these options could allow Mansfield to focus on a more specific set of missions and programs, such as offering the first two years of undergraduate education with transfer to the parent institution for degree completion in some or all degree fields.

By presenting these two specific illustrations, we do not mean to imply that other State System universities not be considered for mergers under Options 2, 3, and 5. Indeed, we recommend that mergers be considered for all State System universities facing significant challenges in enrollment and financial health.

Evaluating the Prospects for the Options

Option 1 appears the simplest to implement because it modifies rather than replaces the current State System structure. In addition, it preserves the historic mission and location of each university. But we think the changes in Option 1 are likely to be less effective at addressing the universities' challenges. Even with changes to Act 188, we do not think change within the system will be adequate to save costs and make weak institutions financially viable. It is likely that these institutions will increase tuition to make ends meet. Because the universities would continue as 14 separate institutions, they would be likely to face continued difficulties in adjusting staffing sizes and programs to match their enrollment prospects.

Option 2 adds some key advantages to Option 1 because regional consolidation of universities would allow them to combine programs regionally and, at least over time, adjust staffing to match enrollment better. They might focus certain programs at certain campuses or focus campuses with weaker demographic prospects on the first two years of undergraduate education, consolidating the third and fourth years at fewer campuses. As a result, we expect Option 2 to generate more cost savings than Option 1, especially over time. By saving costs, at least in the long run, universities are more likely to maintain reasonable tuition and preserve access for students at an affordable price. A key disadvantage is that some universities will lose their mission. In addition, it would be more difficult to implement this option because it requires not only legislative action to modify Act 188 but also resolution of issues regarding institutional debt and labor relations. Processes also must be put in place to ensure that the mergers are done effectively and that the anchor institution's academic standing is not affected.

Option 3 goes further than Option 2, eliminating the State System structure and making these merged universities state-related. This option is likely to give the new universities maximum flexibility in addressing their challenges. But if the new universities do not have sound management or encounter severe external challenges, this option could lead to financial distress and even failure of a university.

Option 4 takes advantage of state-related institutions' strength and capacity, but it does so in a limited way and does not require changing the current universities, their missions, their accreditation, or labor relations, at least initially. This arrangement requires changing the governance structure of the State System institutions so that state-related institutions can operate the business side of the institutions to ensure effective operations and to maximize cost savings. This option has the potential to make weaker institutions financially viable. Although labor agreements could remain largely as they currently are, the new governance structure might enable some revisions of these agreements to give universities more flexibility to adapt to market changes. This arrangement could be reassessed after a certain period of time, such as ten years, to determine whether to keep the arrangement, terminate it, or merge the former State System institutions into state-related universities.

Option 5 also takes advantage of state-related institutions' strength and capacity by merging current State System universities as branch campuses of state-related institutions. This option does risk burdening the state-related institution or institutions with a set of campuses that have declining enrollments and excess physical plant and human resources. Thus, mergers are likely to affect state-related institutions' creditworthiness, while the State System institutions are likely to lose aspects of their current missions. Another significant concern focuses on labor relations; employees would have to transition from the current unionized State System environment to new relationships at state-related institutions. These transitions could result in some employee groups at the state-related institutions becoming unionized or former State System employees moving to nonunion arrangements.

Several of these options could have implications for the sovereign immunity that benefits the State System and its universities as entities of the commonwealth. This immunity protects the system and its universities from many claims and lawsuits. State-related universities do not have this immunity, and some have recently been subject to significant claims, such as those arising at Penn State from the Jerry Sandusky scandal. Options that move State System universities into existing or new state-related institutions will jeopardize this immunity, with potentially significant future risks of claims. Options 1 and 2 that maintain the State System should continue this immunity. We think that Option 4 could maintain the current State System structure and immunity as well, even though that structure would be managed by a state-related institution (although we recognize that the opposite outcome is also possible). Options 5 would mean the end of sovereign immunity for the current State System universities, and Option 3 likely would as well, unless a special arrangement can be made to preserve it.

Should the Commonwealth Establish a Statewide Body to Coordinate or Oversee Higher Education?

As we noted in Chapters One and Two, Pennsylvania has many providers of higher education and most of them—including state-owned, state-related, and private—receive public funding through various streams. In addition, these different providers are competing for a shrinking pool of traditional students. Theoretically, a statewide body with some power to coordinate or oversee these systems and providers could address several concerns with the current arrangements. Such a body could undertake some or all of the following functions:

- Articulate a statewide vision for providing higher education.
- Coordinate funding streams to align with that vision.
- Allocate funding across systems and institutions in a transparent fashion.
- Coordinate discussions about program offerings among institutions with overlapping service areas and degree programs.
- Approve new degree programs (or those that meet specified criteria).

- Approve the establishment of new branch campus or teaching sites.
- Approve mergers of state-owned or state-related institutions.
- Offer selected shared services to institutions that would like to subscribe to them.

Other states with multiple systems of publicly supported institutions, such as Ohio and Texas, have adopted such coordinating boards or agencies with some or all of these functions. In Texas, for example, the Texas Higher Education Coordinating Board has, in our experience, served a useful mediating function among multiple public systems of higher education. But it also generates frictions with and among these systems and, in response to these frictions, the legislature has reduced the level and scope of authorities for the coordinating board over time.

Despite the theoretical benefits of such a body, almost all of the leadership stakeholders we interviewed within the State System and state-related institutions argued that such a statewide body would add more layers of approval. And, because state-related and private institutions enjoy considerable autonomy, they might oppose the development of a new state body that assumes some authority over them.

Given these stakeholder arguments and the concerns about existing governance arrangements expressed in Chapter Three, we generally caution against establishment of a new statewide body in addition to current arrangements. However, there is a sounder argument for a new statewide body that replaces current structures. In that vein, we note under Option 3 that the state might wish to constitute a coordinating body for at least some functions, such as allocation of state appropriations. The state also might wish to establish a nonbinding discussion forum where universities can come together to discuss aspects of strategy that overlap, such as program offerings and campus locations. We do not expect that such a forum would make a major improvement in coordination, but it could help universities and systems coordinate more effectively.

Chapter Six
Conclusion and Recommendations

This report highlights the external and internal challenges that the State System and its universities face. As discussed, significant challenges arise from long-term shifts in the population, strong competition, limited state funding, and internal structures within the State System that are poorly designed for adapting to these challenges. Thus, we do not see a continuation of the current system as likely to address the challenges; major structural changes are needed.

Even significant changes to the current State System structure as outlined in Option 1 are likely to be inadequate to address the challenges in a comprehensive, long-term fashion. As discussed, even if Act 188 is modified to change governance, reallocate authority across the State System and its institutions so it is more balanced, and increase accountability, the system will remain divided into 14 separate universities, limiting their ability to adjust staffing and programs in response to enrollment trends.

Given the considerable uncertainties involved in all the options, especially Options 2–5, we cannot be sure which option has the strongest chance of making the current universities more sustainable. Based on the limited prospects we see for Option 1, we think the state should seriously consider other structural change options. These options are likely to be more difficult to implement and could entail other risks. In particular, options where the current State System universities become independent state-related universities or merge with state-related institutions could result in the loss of the State System's valuable sovereign immunity from lawsuits and might lead to increases in student costs. But if any of Options 2–5 are implemented well, they are likely to meet key objectives of strengthening financially weak institutions and better matching staffing size to enrollment trends.

Options 2, 3, and 5 propose mergers, which could be an approach for cost savings by matching financially weak institutions with stronger ones and by allowing institutions more flexibility to reallocate programs and staffing across campuses to make all campuses more viable. However, institutions (especially ones facing significant challenges) are likely to lose aspects of their current missions. In addition, anchor institutions could lose their academic standing and incur more debt if the state does not provide support.

The implementation of mergers is quite complex, not only because of the need to modify or repeal Act 188 and other laws, but also because these options—specifically making regional mergers independent of the State System (Option 3) and merging with state-related institutions (Option 5)—would require negotiating new labor agreements and coordination among institutions and with accreditors. As we noted in Chapter Five, many mergers have failed to deliver on their promised benefits, so these options definitely involve some risks.

49

Making State System institutions subsidiary to a large state-related institution balances structural changes, feasibility of implementation, and associated risks (Option 4). The state-related institution governs and oversees the administrative functioning of the State System institutions to ensure efficiency and maximize savings while the institutions control their educational operations. Institutions do not lose their missions and we expect the State System Board's accountability function to be strengthened by the control of the state-related university. Although this option requires legislative action, it mostly pertains to modifying Act 188. Labor agreements could continue in force, perhaps with future adjustments negotiated between the system and unions, aimed at increasing flexibility. This option does not entail the complexities of mergers, and it would also require state-committed funding. We view this requirement as feasible because it will not require the state to provide more than it already does to State System institutions.

At this stage, we do not know whether the large state-related institutions would be seriously interested in Option 4 (state-related control) or Option 5 (merger as branch campuses) or have a preference between these options. We think these two options have the best long-term prospects and recommend either of them, if one or more willing partners can be found among the state-related institutions. From the state-related institutions' perspectives, each of these two options has strengths and weaknesses. Option 4 isolates the State System universities from the state-related system and does not require major adjustments to labor arrangements or mergers. Option 5 requires addressing both labor and mergers, but it might have a long-run advantage because the state-related institutions could reallocate programs and resources across a wider span of campuses.

If the state and one or more large state-related institutions cannot reach an agreement to implement either Option 4 or 5, then the state should consider mergers, such as Options 2 or 3. As we noted in Chapter Five, it is possible to use more than one of these options, rather than treating all 14 current State System universities the same.

If none of Options 2–5 appears feasible, we recommend that the state pursue Option 1 as a final choice, revising the State System's structure. We do think this option will improve prospects for the current State System universities but probably not to a degree sufficient to address their long-term challenges.

We recommend that under any of the options, the universities should be granted greater autonomy in the areas of procurement and construction, either by amending the relevant laws or by selecting options where these laws do not apply.

Finally, the state could theoretically benefit from a coordinating body to align the activities of its diverse set of higher education providers. But because of our concerns about the additional layers of bureaucracy and the difficulty in getting political support from the major higher education sectors, we advise against establishing such a body unless it is necessary for a specific purpose under one of the options selected, such as the need to distribute state higher education funding according to an agreed-on formula.

This project was conducted through five broad and interrelated tasks that consisted of both quantitative and qualitative analysis. We describe each of the tasks here.

Task 1. Review and analyze the NCHEMS and other relevant reports. We began the project by reviewing the 2017 NCHEMS report commissioned by the State System. Other relevant reports regarding the fiscal, demographic, and management challenges faced by State System universities were reviewed at this early stage. These included the State System universities' action plans and budget documents from the General Assembly.

Task 2. Review other states' policies and governance arrangements. The team reviewed a sample of other states that have higher education systems larger than or comparable to that of Pennsylvania in terms of size and breadth—specifically, Maine, Maryland, New York, North Carolina, Texas, Ohio, and California. The research team examined these states' policies and structures for public higher education and how these and other states have managed or are addressing challenges similar to those that the State System faces. The team also reviewed faculty collective bargaining agreements from Maine, New York, California, and New Jersey. In conducting this task, we also conducted telephone interviews, typically one hour in length, with the following:

- four observers and participants in state systems of other states, including one union leader (in addition to a series of relevant interviews in four other states that members of our team conducted for other research projects)
- two academic experts in higher education labor relations.

Task 3. Analyze Pennsylvania higher education using statistical data. This task required the extensive compilation and analysis of data from the IPEDS System, the CO, the Pennsylvania State Data Center, and the General Assembly. The research team used these sources to project trends in the population seeking higher education and a variety of trends in enrollment, staffing, and finance for the State System and other institutions in the state.

Task 4. Solicit and review input from Pennsylvania stakeholders. To examine the support and feasibility of each option, the team reviewed the extensive stakeholder consultations reported in the 2017 NCHEMS report, and supplemented this material with additional stakeholder interviews. The team made one-day site visits to four State System universities: California, Cheyney, Mansfield, and Slippery Rock. We selected these four because they span a range of greater and lesser declines in enrollment and resulting financial challenges and because they cover different regions of the state. During each visit, we toured the campus and surrounding community and conducted discussions with the following groups:

- a leadership group (at least the president, chief academic officer, and chief financial officer, and often other officers of the president's choice)
- a group of up to four trustees, including the chair of the COT and other members of the chair's selection
- a group of four to eight elected student government leaders
- a group of approximately six faculty (whom we randomly selected from all full-time faculty at the institution)
- a group of approximately six student services staff (whom we randomly selected from a common set of student service functions).

We also conducted telephone interviews, typically one hour in length with the following:

- the leadership of the other ten State System universities not selected for visits (typically the president, chief academic officer, and chief financial officer)
- the leadership of the four state-related universities (typically the president but sometimes other leaders as well)
- the leadership of two major unions representing State System employees
- a group of leaders from State System university-affiliated foundations
- two Republican state legislators (we extended invitations to a total of ten members, about equally divided between Republicans and Democrats—specifically the House and Senate education majority and minority leaders, the four legislators who sit on the Board of Governors, and two additional major proponents of the resolution commissioning this study).

Task 5. Analyze alternative policies and implementation requirements. Based on the information collected in tasks 2, 3, and 4, we developed a set of options, assessed the pros and cons of each option, and evaluated each option's feasibility—taking into account implementation requirements and changes that need to take place in laws, policies, regulations, and structures of the system and its governing bodies. We were able to recommend options and actions that the state, the university system, and universities can take to strengthen the system, and we examined one or more statewide structures that could coordinate better across Pennsylvania's postsecondary sector.

Appendix B
Detailed Tables and Graphs

Table B.1. Projected Population by County, Age 15–19 Years, Pennsylvania, 2015–2030 (Sorted in Descending Order of Growth)

County	2015	2020	2025	2030	Change 2015 to 2030 (%)
Sullivan County	477	456	513	607	27.3
Philadelphia County	109,509	110,688	122,752	135,225	23.5
Montour County	1,195	1,305	1,356	1,473	23.3
Lancaster County	40,442	40,787	41,447	42,355	4.7
Indiana County	9,222	9,934	10,699	9,486	2.9
Mifflin County	3,013	2,877	2,796	3,098	2.8
Blair County	8,450	8,514	8,503	8,559	1.3
Franklin County	10,789	10,514	10,871	10,895	1.0
Allegheny County	83,932	81,224	82,481	84,440	0.6
Dauphin County	17,473	16,440	16,473	17,570	0.6
Clinton County	4,116	4,459	4,861	4,103	−0.3
Cameron County	296	237	218	288	−2.7
Erie County	22,806	22,112	22,137	22,102	−3.1
Perry County	3,102	2,868	2,775	2,992	−3.5
Schuylkill County	8,858	8,562	8,179	8,521	−3.8
Lackawanna County	15,026	14,444	14,501	14,337	−4.6
Jefferson County	2,893	2,756	2,653	2,760	−4.6
Berks County	33,062	32,861	31,800	31,508	−4.7
Tioga County	3,254	3,169	3,162	3,094	−4.9
Centre County	17,608	18,544	19,992	16,732	−5.0
Delaware County	44,969	43,037	42,654	42,195	−6.2
Luzerne County	21,211	20,244	19,702	19,833	−6.5
Cumberland County	18,853	18,925	18,962	17,615	−6.6
Beaver County	10,666	10,097	9,855	9,881	−7.4
Lebanon County	9,164	8,881	8,815	8,481	−7.5
Northumberland County	5,487	5,379	5,287	5,069	−7.6
Cambria County	10,044	9,894	9,575	9,276	−7.6
Bradford County	4,089	3,707	3,688	3,772	−7.8
Union County	4,228	4,633	4,546	3,896	−7.9
York County	30,825	29,984	28,376	28,316	−8.1
Clarion County	3,886	3,988	4,435	3,550	−8.6
Venango County	3,588	3,253	3,226	3,256	−9.3
Lehigh County	25,719	24,617	23,496	23,339	−9.3
Columbia County	6,758	6,911	7,081	6,091	−9.9
Lycoming County	8,301	8,198	7,987	7,443	−10.3

County	2015	2020	2025	2030	Change 2015 to 2030 (%)
Northampton County	22,865	22,625	21,269	20,388	−10.8
Montgomery County	56,089	53,050	49,881	49,951	−10.9
Greene County	2,753	2,656	2,500	2,445	−11.2
Fulton County	1,040	947	967	920	−11.5
Snyder County	3,451	3,613	3,621	3,052	−11.6
McKean County	3,206	3,043	2,973	2,829	−11.8
Mercer County	9,801	9,500	9,110	8,481	−13.5
Chester County	41,260	40,492	36,926	35,674	−13.5
Fayette County	8,256	7,484	6,863	7,109	−13.9
Carbon County	4,068	3,869	3,703	3,476	−14.6
Huntingdon County	3,373	3,170	3,245	2,873	−14.8
Wyoming County	2,049	1,889	1,786	1,744	−14.9
Crawford County	6,946	6,530	6,277	5,869	−15.5
Potter County	1,082	955	866	907	−16.2
Forest County	521	481	449	436	−16.3
Adams County	7,784	7,482	7,086	6,511	−16.4
Bedford County	3,236	2,967	2,674	2,700	−16.6
Armstrong County	4,071	3,445	3,317	3,356	−17.6
Somerset County	4,579	4,149	3,761	3,759	−17.9
Butler County	14,621	13,621	12,304	11,994	−18.0
Lawrence County	6,242	5,789	5,557	5,114	−18.1
Washington County	14,331	13,460	12,376	11,688	−18.4
Juniata County	1,625	1,568	1,417	1,302	−19.9
Westmoreland County	22,768	20,367	18,708	18,098	−20.5
Clearfield County	4,821	4,241	3,904	3,791	−21.4
Elk County	1,940	1,657	1,392	1,483	−23.6
Warren County	2,527	2,213	1,932	1,891	−25.2
Wayne County	3,130	2,592	2,096	2,341	−25.2
Bucks County	44,127	39,265	34,275	32,556	−26.2
Susquehanna County	2,661	2,193	1,925	1,864	−30.0
Monroe County	14,319	12,257	10,460	9,526	−33.5
Pike County	4,126	3,362	2,670	2,266	−45.1
Pennsylvania Total	**926,979**	**895,431**	**882,144**	**878,552**	**−5.2**

SOURCE: Pennsylvania State Data Center, 2012.
NOTE: Pennsylvania State Data Center's 2015 estimates for the 15- to 19-year-old cohort (produced in 2012) might not match more recent estimates of population from the U.S. Census Bureau. Long-term growth rates through 2030 for these cohorts by county are still the basis for demographic projections in the Commonwealth of Pennsylvania and are used by state agencies and in the budget process.

Table B.2. State System University Enrollment Areas and Projected Population Change, Ages 15–19 Years, 2015–2030

2016 Enrollment—Top Counties			2015–2030 Youth Population Forecast	
University	**Students**	**Percentage**	**Region**	**Change, 2015–2030**
Bloomsburg				
Columbia	850	9.7%	Surrounding counties	
Philadelphia	691	7.9%	Columbia	−9.9%
Montgomery	661	7.6%	Luzerne	−6.5%
Bucks	628	7.2%	Northumberland	−7.6%
Luzerne	605	6.9%	Weighted Average	−8.2%
Northumberland	572	6.6%	Other regions	
Delaware	391	4.5%	Philadelphia metropolitan area	−0.1%
Total	4,398	50.4%		
California				
Allegheny	1,697	26.9%	Surrounding counties	
Washington	1,106	17.5%	Allegheny	0.6%
Fayette	865	13.7%	Washington	−18.4%
Total	3,668	58.1%	Fayette	−13.9%
			Weighted Average	−3.1%
			Other regions	
			Pittsburgh metropolitan area	−7.6%
Cheyney				
Philadelphia	306	59.4%	Surrounding counties	
Delaware	90	17.5%	Philadelphia	23.5%
Chester	27	5.2%	Delaware	−6.2%
Total	423	82.1%	Chester	−13.5%
			Weighted Average	14.8%
			Other regions	
			Philadelphia metropolitan area	−0.1%
Clarion				
Clarion	651	14.0%	Surrounding counties	
Allegheny	639	13.8%	Clarion	−8.6%
Venango	426	9.2%	Venango	−9.3%
Jefferson	229	4.9%	Jefferson	−4.6%
Butler	217	4.7%	Mercer	−13.5%
Mercer	187	4.0%	Weighted Average	−8.8%
Total	2,349	50.6%	Other regions	
			Pittsburgh metropolitan area	−7.6%

2016 Enrollment—Top Counties			2015–2030 Youth Population Forecast	
University	Students	Percentage	Region	Change, 2015–2030
East Stroudsburg				
Monroe	1,634	30.6%	Surrounding counties	
Northampton	813	15.2%	Monroe	−33.5%
Philadelphia	444	8.3%	Northampton	−10.8%
Total	2,891	54.2%	Weighted Average	−26.0%
			Other regions	
			Philadelphia metropolitan area	−0.1%
Edinboro				
Erie	2,323	44.9%	Surrounding counties	
Crawford	543	10.5%	Erie	−3.1%
Allegheny	518	10.0%	Crawford	−15.5%
Total	3,384	65.4%	Weighted Average	−5.4%
			Other regions	
			Pittsburgh metropolitan area	−7.6%
Indiana				
Allegheny	1,594	14.4%	Surrounding counties	
Indiana	1,375	12.4%	Indiana	2.9%
Westmoreland	955	8.6%	Cambria	−7.6%
Philadelphia	663	6.0%	Weighted Average	−0.5%
Cambria	639	5.8%	Other regions	
Butler	358	3.2%	Pittsburgh metropolitan area	−7.6%
Total	5,584	50.4%	Philadelphia metropolitan area	−0.1%
Kutztown				
Berks	1,465	19.4%	Surrounding counties	
Lehigh	1,038	13.7%	Berks	−4.7%
Montgomery	775	10.2%	Lehigh	−9.3%
Bucks	535	7.1%	Weighted Average	−6.6%
Total	3,813	50.4%	Other regions	
			Philadelphia metropolitan area	−0.1%

2016 Enrollment—Top Counties			2015–2030 Youth Population Forecast	
University	Students	Percentage	Region	Change, 2015–2030
Lock Haven				
Clinton	484	12.2%	Surrounding counties	
Centre	380	9.6%	Clinton	–0.3%
Lycoming	366	9.2%	Centre	–5.0%
Clearfield	339	8.6%	Lycoming	–10.3%
Philadelphia	181	4.6%	Clearfield	–21.4%
York	135	3.4%	Weighted Average	–8.3%
Lancaster	128	3.2%	Other regions	
Total	2,013	50.8%	Philadelphia metropolitan area	–0.1%
			Lancaster–York–Hanover metropolitan area	–0.8%
Mansfield				
Tioga	361	20.1%	Surrounding counties	
Bradford	295	16.4%	Tioga	–4.9%
Philadelphia	146	8.1%	Bradford	–7.8%
Lycoming	122	6.8%	Lycoming	–10.3%
Total	924	51.4%	Weighted Average	–8.5%
			Other regions	
			Philadelphia metropolitan area	–0.1%
Millersville				
Lancaster	2,748	37.0%	Surrounding counties	
York	946	12.7%	Lancaster	4.7%
Chester	476	6.4%	York	–8.1%
Total	4,170	56.1%	Weighted Average	1.4%
			Other regions	
			Philadelphia metropolitan area	–0.1%
Shippensburg				
Cumberland	1,015	16.0%	Surrounding counties	
Franklin	983	15.5%	Cumberland	–6.6%
York	483	7.6%	Franklin	1.0%
Dauphin	377	5.9%	York	–8.1%
Montgomery	355	5.6%	Dauphin	0.6%
Total	3,213	50.5%	Weighted Average	–3.3%
			Other regions	
			Philadelphia metropolitan area	–0.1%

2016 Enrollment—Top Counties			2015–2030 Youth Population Forecast	
University	Students	Percentage	Region	Change, 2015–2030
Slippery Rock				
Allegheny	1,931	24.7%	Surrounding counties	
Butler	1,152	14.7%	Allegheny County	0.6%
Mercer	522	6.7%	Butler County	−18.0%
Beaver	505	6.4%	Mercer County	−13.5%
Total	4,110	52.5%	Beaver County	−7.4%
			Weighted Average	−7.4%
			Other regions	
			Pittsburgh metropolitan area	−7.6%
West Chester				
Chester	4,139	27.3%	Surrounding counties	
Delaware	2,664	17.6%	Chester County	−13.5%
Montgomery	2,104	13.9%	Delaware County	−6.2%
Total	8,907	58.8%	Montgomery County	−10.9%
			Weighted Average	−10.7%
			Other regions	
			Philadelphia metropolitan area	−0.1%

SOURCE: RAND calculations from enrollment regions from the CO and projections in Pennsylvania State Data Center, 2012.
NOTE: Surrounding counties averages are weighted by 2016 enrollment percentages.

Figure B.1. Location of State System and State-Related Universities in Pennsylvania

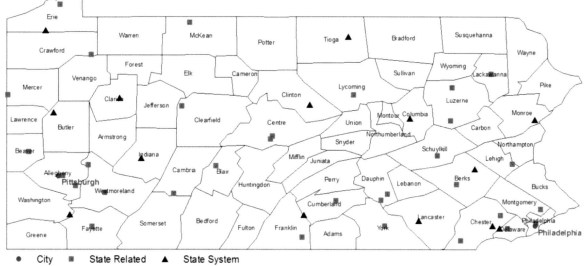

● City   ■ State Related   ▲ State System

SOURCE: National Center for Education Statistics, undated.

Table B.3. Total Degrees Awarded by Broad Field and Sector, 2006–2016

Subject Area/Sector	2006	2007	2008	2009	2010	2011	2012	2013	2014	2015	2016	2010–2016 Change (%)
Business												
State System	2,994	3,278	3,201	3,599	3,728	3,688	3,573	3,542	3,661	3,898	4,111	10.3
State-related	6,222	5,982	5,982	6,422	7,070	6,911	6,755	6,548	6,958	7,078	7,716	9.1
Community colleges	2,004	2,106	2,201	2,323	2,259	2,324	2,362	2,268	2,301	2,301	2,277	0.8
Four-year private	13,226	13,204	13,088	13,370	13,857	13,771	13,503	13,268	13,451	13,661	13,735	−0.9
Education												
State System	4,525	4,619	4,496	4,684	4,762	4,729	5,019	4,212	3,651	3,306	3,138	−34.1
State-related	2,701	2,808	2,616	2,415	2,563	2,432	2,530	2,143	2,063	1,905	1,745	−31.9
Community colleges	840	850	857	880	881	893	758	661	605	567	550	−37.6
Four-year private	7,142	7,440	7,561	8,130	8,181	8,863	8,676	8,129	6,890	6,151	5,962	−27.1
Engineering												
State System	391	343	419	451	469	510	513	490	499	486	511	9.0
State-related	3,634	3,595	3,729	3,625	3,714	3,882	4,079	4,259	4,543	4,565	5,069	36.5
Community colleges	613	567	539	537	595	680	726	657	696	602	695	16.8
Four-year private	3,216	3,494	3,698	3,924	4,179	4,014	4,413	4,746	4,933	5,402	5,683	36.0
Fine arts												
State System	1,156	1,234	1,177	1,168	1,152	1,215	1,245	1,185	1,174	1,189	1,040	−9.7
State-related	1,261	1,242	1,154	1,246	1,375	1,327	1,416	1,311	1,220	1,104	1,025	−25.5
Community colleges	351	394	381	379	353	406	458	436	534	544	609	72.5
Four-year private	2,017	2,170	2,164	2,404	2,395	2,394	2,585	2,544	2,595	2,502	2,547	6.3
Health												
State System	1,762	1,902	2,034	2,206	2,134	2,441	2,784	2,979	3,092	3,290	3,553	66.5
State-related	3,511	3,749	3,756	3,927	4,301	4,613	4,758	5,052	5,156	5,257	5,483	27.5
Community colleges	2,507	2,475	2,671	2,767	2,813	2,853	3,092	2,992	3,082	2,943	2,950	4.9
Four-year private	6,441	7,155	7,707	8,377	8,798	9,320	9,738	10,510	10,776	11,739	11,891	35.2

Subject Area/ Sector	2006	2007	2008	2009	2010	2011	2012	2013	2014	2015	2016	2010–2016 Change (%)
Legal												
State System	37	56	61	55	72	70	52	62	47	55	55	−23.6
State-related	1,006	960	989	985	955	1,029	925	944	897	844	753	−21.2
Community colleges	202	246	227	213	217	250	241	233	226	191	164	−24.4
Four-year private	822	825	777	993	952	989	1,036	995	1,002	955	1,244	30.7
Liberal arts												
State System	4,575	4,845	4,946	5,171	5,148	5,216	5,459	5,779	5,704	5,682	5,321	3.4
State-related	5,486	5,533	5,599	5,731	6,064	6,086	6,198	5,997	6,051	5,831	5,573	−8.1
Community colleges	2,429	2,671	2,826	3,014	3,126	3,350	3,499	3,731	3,847	3,830	3,762	20.3
Four-year private	8,924	9,158	9,513	9,886	9,494	9,573	9,479	9,413	9,365	8,729	8,094	−14.7
Science												
State System	1,820	1,821	1,889	1,869	1,898	1,978	2,062	2,315	2,359	2,445	2,297	21.0
State-related	4,137	4,057	4,018	4,262	4,599	5,007	5,041	5,425	5,771	5,848	6,079	32.2
Community colleges	590	597	575	568	652	844	924	913	940	942	999	53.2
Four-year private	6,410	6,285	6,677	6,663	7,378	7,588	7,969	8,366	9,067	9,395	9,623	30.4
Social science												
State System	4,314	4,422	4,420	4,688	4,668	4,866	4,906	5,280	5,512	5,418	5,179	10.9
State-related	6,036	6,016	6,281	6,199	6,618	6,832	7,097	7,207	7,572	7,344	6,969	5.3
Community colleges	1,545	1,629	1,677	1,568	1,613	1,700	2,065	2,088	2,133	2,061	2,018	25.1
Four-year private	8,825	8,926	9,286	9,474	9,230	9,679	9,889	10,249	10,124	10,002	9,838	6.6

SOURCE: National Center for Education Statistics, undated.

NOTE: Discipline clusters defined by RAND based on the Classification of Instructional Programs.

Table B.4. Undergraduate In-State Tuition and Fees by Sector ($), 2007–2016

Sector	2007	2008	2009	2010	2011	2012	2013	2014	2015	2016	Average Annual Growth Rate
State System	6,731	7,066	7,338	7,720	8,361	8,646	8,963	9,293	9,655	9,990	4.5%
State-related main campus	11,844	12,596	13,070	13,804	14,925	15,155	15,629	16,404	16,656	17,107	4.2%
State-related branch campus	11,006	11,718	12,200	12,684	13,048	13,350	13,533	13,904	13,938	14,107	2.8%
Community college	5,640	5,880	6,035	6,180	6,630	6,870	7,184	7,410	7,890	8,370	4.5%
Four-year private	25,397	26,747	27,643	28,645	29,742	30,760	31,728	32,698	33,882	35,350	3.7%

SOURCE: National Center for Education Statistics, undated.
NOTE: The table reports the median of institutional values by sector.

Table B.5. On Campus Room and Board by Sector ($), 2007–2016

Sector	2007	2008	2009	2010	2011	2012	2013	2014	2015	2016	Average Annual Growth Rate
State System	6,258	6,611	7,414	8,196	8,326	8,872	9,254	9,940	10,161	11,183	6.7%
State-related main campus	8,020	8,431	8,860	9,142	9,431	9,786	10,206	10,643	10,913	11,090	3.7%
State-related branch campus	7,740	8,262	8,820	9,054	9,432	9,702	10,116	10,548	10,926	11,230	4.2%
Community college	5,972	6,579	7,131	7,358	7,652	7,888	8,099	8,340	8,296	8,613	4.2%
Four-year private	8,515	8,894	9,285	9,630	10,074	10,379	10,792	11,162	11,720	11,995	3.9%

SOURCE: National Center for Education Statistics, undated.
NOTE: The table reports the median of institutional values by sector.

Table B.6. Six-Year Graduation Rates by Sector and National Averages, 2006 and 2016 (percentage)

Sector	2006	2016
State System	54.2	56.6
State-related	65.6	69.6
Four-year private	72.9	73.7
National averages		
Public, four-year	53.3	54.7
Private nonprofit, Four-year	63.8	64.0
Private for-profit, Four-year	48.2	27.9

SOURCE: National Center for Education Statistics, undated.
National averages from IPEDS Trend Generator.
NOTE: Rates measure the percentage of first-time bachelor's
seeking institutions that graduate within the specified period
from the same institution.

Table B.7. Six-Year Graduation Rates at State System Universities, 2006 and 2016 (percentage)

University	2006	2016
Bloomsburg	65	62
California	50	54
Cheyney	29	16
Clarion	52	50
East Stroudsburg	52	57
Edinboro	49	49
Indiana	49	54
Kutztown	52	55
Lock Haven	53	48
Mansfield	48	54
Millersville	63	61
Shippensburg	63	56
Slippery Rock	52	68
West Chester	59	70

SOURCE: National Center for Education Statistics,
undated.
NOTE: Rates measure the percentage of first-time
bachelor's seeking institutions that graduate within the
specified period from the same institution.

Table B.8. Students and Staffing at State System Universities, 2010–2016

University	Students (Fall FTE)		Instructional Staff (FTE)		Non-instructional Staff (FTE)		Change 2010–2016 (%)		
	2010	2016	2010	2016	2010	2016	Students	Instructional Staff	Noninstructional Staff
Bloomsburg	9,457	9,011	432	443	576	605	−4.7	2.6	5.2
California	8,372	6,242	308	309	538	427	−25.4	0.3	−20.6
Cheyney	1,457	705	88	58	200	112	−51.6	−33.5	−44.1
Clarion	6,225	4,345	290	230	398	380	−30.2	−20.9	−4.5
East Stroudsburg	6,656	6,278	321	301	468	399	−5.7	−6.3	−14.7
Edinboro	7,351	5,436	363	298	414	381	−26.0	−18.1	−7.8
Indiana	13,738	11,753	651	642	835	810	−14.4	−1.3	−3.0
Kutztown	9,784	7,927	443	424	571	529	−19.0	−4.4	−7.2
Lock Haven	5,116	3,937	235	213	334	302	−23.0	−9.5	−9.7
Mansfield	3,054	2,027	173	151	255	217	−33.6	−12.9	−14.8
Millersville	7,796	6,826	342	360	574	544	−12.4	5.3	−5.2
Shippensburg	7,564	6,303	357	315	481	459	−16.7	−11.8	−4.7
Slippery Rock	8,256	8,087	373	367	517	501	−2.1	−1.6	−3.0
West Chester	12,904	14,971	623	776	782	863	16.0	24.6	10.3

SOURCE: National Center for Education Statistics, undated.

Financial Indicators

Approximated cash flow is derived from IPEDS financial data by adding depreciation and interest to change in net position. Although a true cash flow measure might also add a few other items, IPEDS does not have separate variables for these and we expect that they are generally small in the context of higher education. In approximated cash flow, larger values are financially healthier for institutions. For long-term debt, it is considered healthier to have a higher ratio of estimated cash flow to long-term debt, and a lower ratio of long-term debt to total revenues. As shown in Figures B.2–B.4, all three of these indicators are generally worsening over time, although some universities are faring much better than others. Tables B.9–B.12 provide the data points graphed in the figures.

Figure B.2. Estimated Cash Flow, Three-Year Average at State System Universities, 2006–2008 to 2014–2016

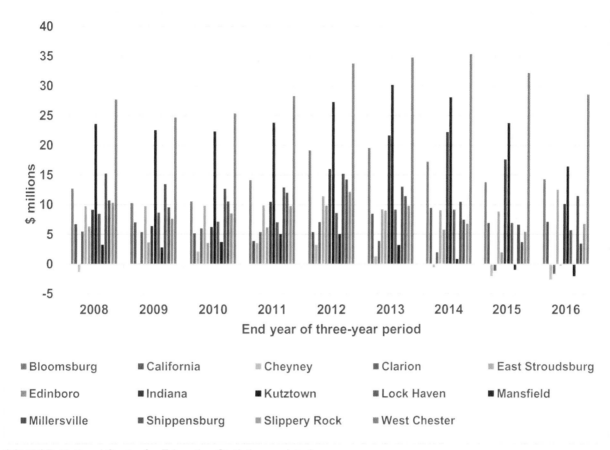

SOURCE: National Center for Education Statistics, undated.
NOTE: Each bar represents one of the 14 State System universities, shown in alphabetical order. All adjustments to net position, such as one-time changes in liabilities, are excluded.

Figure B.3. Ratio of Estimated Cash Flow to Long-Term Debt, Three-Year Average at State System Universities, 2006–2008 to 2014–2016

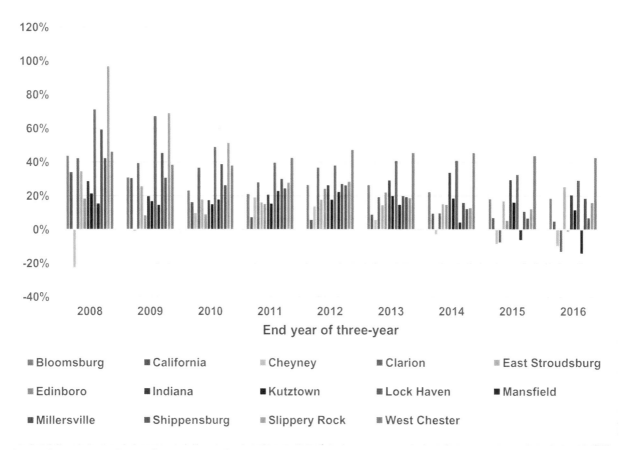

SOURCE: National Center for Education Statistics, undated.

NOTE: Each bar represents one of the 14 State System universities, shown in alphabetical order.

Figure B.4. Ratio of Estimated Long-Term Debt to Total Revenues, Three-Year Average at State System Universities, 2006–2008 to 2014–2016

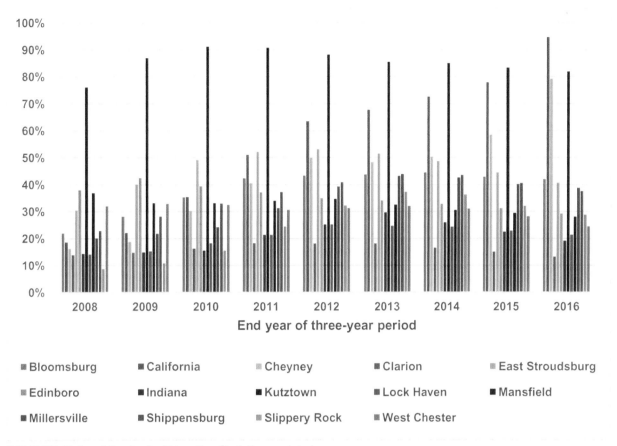

SOURCE: National Center for Education Statistics, undated.

NOTE: Each bar represents one of the 14 State System universities, shown in alphabetical order.

Table B.9. Change in Net Position (Surplus or Deficit), Three-Year Average at State System Universities, 2006–2008 to 2014–2016 ($million)

University	Three-Year Period Ending in								
	2008	**2009**	**2010**	**2011**	**2012**	**2013**	**2014**	**2015**	**2016**
Bloomsburg	5.2	2.1	1.2	3.4	6.8	6.5	3.5	0.0	−0.2
California	3.0	3.0	0.7	−1.5	−1.8	−0.7	−1.3	−4.2	−5.8
Cheyney	−3.0	−2.0	−0.5	0.5	−0.1	−2.3	−4.4	−5.8	−6.3
Clarion	1.2	1.0	1.3	0.3	1.9	−1.4	−3.3	−6.5	−7.0
East Stroudsburg	5.0	4.0	2.9	1.4	2.2	−0.6	−1.0	−0.8	3.2
Edinboro	−0.7	−4.5	−5.7	−3.9	−0.3	−1.0	−3.5	−6.3	−7.5
Indiana	−2.0	−5.1	−5.6	−1.8	2.9	8.0	7.7	3.7	−3.4
Kutztown	10.4	7.5	5.7	5.6	8.0	9.4	5.8	0.6	−7.0
Lock Haven	4.6	4.2	2.0	1.5	2.9	3.5	3.6	1.3	0.1
Mansfield	−0.6	−1.1	−0.3	0.6	0.4	−1.6	−3.9	−5.6	−6.5
Millersville	6.9	4.1	2.9	2.8	4.0	1.1	−2.5	−7.5	−4.0
Shippensburg	3.0	1.3	1.6	2.4	4.2	0.6	−4.2	−8.3	−8.2
Slippery Rock	5.3	2.5	2.8	3.0	4.1	0.6	−2.7	−4.0	−2.4
West Chester	13.9	9.5	9.4	12.6	18.4	19.4	19.1	15.1	10.7

SOURCE: National Center for Education Statistics, undated. All adjustments to net position, such as one-time changes in liabilities, are excluded.

Table B.10. Estimated Cash Flow, Three-Year Average at State System Universities, 2006–2008 to 2014–2016 ($million)

University	Three-Year Period Ending in								
	2008	**2009**	**2010**	**2011**	**2012**	**2013**	**2014**	**2015**	**2016**
Bloomsburg	12.8	10.3	10.5	14.1	19.2	19.5	17.2	13.8	14.3
California	6.7	7.0	5.2	3.9	5.4	8.5	9.5	6.9	7.2
Cheyney	−1.4	0.1	2.2	3.6	3.3	1.3	−0.6	−2.0	−2.6
Clarion	5.5	5.4	6.0	5.4	7.1	3.9	2.0	−1.1	−1.6
East Stroudsburg	9.8	9.8	9.8	9.9	11.5	9.2	9.1	8.9	12.6
Edinboro	6.4	3.7	3.5	6.2	9.9	9.0	5.8	2.0	−0.2
Indiana	9.2	6.4	6.2	10.5	16.0	21.7	22.2	17.6	10.2
Kutztown	23.7	22.6	22.3	23.8	27.3	30.1	28.1	23.8	16.5
Lock Haven	8.5	8.7	7.1	7.0	8.6	9.2	9.2	6.9	5.8
Mansfield	3.3	2.8	3.7	5.1	5.1	3.2	0.9	−0.9	−2.0
Millersville	15.3	13.5	12.7	12.9	15.2	13.0	10.5	6.6	11.5
Shippensburg	10.8	9.5	10.6	12.0	14.3	11.5	7.5	3.7	3.5
Slippery Rock	10.3	7.6	8.5	9.8	12.2	9.8	6.8	5.5	6.8
West Chester	27.7	24.7	25.4	28.3	33.8	34.8	35.4	32.2	28.6

SOURCE: National Center for Education Statistics, undated. All adjustments to net position, such as one-time changes in liabilities, are excluded.

67

Table B.11. Ratio of Estimated Cash Flow to Long-Term Debt, Three-Year Average at State System Universities, 2006–2008 to 2014–2016 (percentage)

University									
	Three-Year Period Ending in								
University	**2008**	**2009**	**2010**	**2011**	**2012**	**2013**	**2014**	**2015**	**2016**
Bloomsburg	43.7	30.9	23.2	21.2	26.6	26.4	22.3	18.3	18.6
California	34.0	30.5	16.3	7.3	5.8	8.8	9.6	6.9	5.0
Cheyney	−22.5	−0.9	9.7	19.1	14.0	5.7	−2.7	−8.6	−9.7
Clarion	42.3	39.3	36.6	28.2	36.8	19.4	9.6	−7.5	−13.0
East Stroudsburg	34.7	25.7	17.9	16.3	17.9	14.6	15.2	17.1	25.6
Edinboro	18.4	8.3	8.8	15.2	24.3	22.1	14.9	5.4	−1.1
Indiana	28.6	19.8	17.4	20.7	26.3	29.3	33.9	29.4	20.5
Kutztown	21.3	16.9	15.0	15.5	17.8	19.9	18.7	16.3	11.6
Lock Haven	71.3	67.3	48.8	39.5	38.1	40.8	41.0	32.6	29.4
Mansfield	15.5	14.6	17.9	22.9	22.3	14.8	4.5	−6.1	−14.0
Millersville	59.3	45.3	38.8	30.1	27.1	20.1	16.1	10.8	18.5
Shippensburg	42.4	30.7	26.4	24.6	26.3	19.5	12.3	6.8	7.0
Slippery Rock	96.9	69.1	51.4	28.0	28.5	18.8	12.8	12.2	16.0
West Chester	46.2	38.4	37.9	42.6	47.2	45.6	45.5	43.8	42.7

SOURCE: National Center for Education Statistics, undated.

Table B.12. Ratio of Estimated Long-Term Debt to Total Revenues, Three-Year Average at State System Universities, 2006–2008 to 2014–2016 (percentage)

University									
	Three-Year Period Ending in								
University	**2008**	**2009**	**2010**	**2011**	**2012**	**2013**	**2014**	**2015**	**2016**
Bloomsburg	21.9	28.1	35.3	42.3	43.3	43.7	44.4	42.8	41.9
California	18.6	22.1	35.4	51.0	63.4	67.6	72.5	77.7	94.6
Cheyney	16.2	18.9	30.2	40.5	49.9	48.2	50.2	58.4	79.1
Clarion	13.9	14.8	16.2	18.2	18.1	18.1	16.5	15.0	13.1
East Stroudsburg	30.4	40.1	49.1	52.0	53.1	51.5	48.6	44.4	40.6
Edinboro	38.0	42.5	39.3	37.1	34.9	34.0	32.7	31.1	29.0
Indiana	14.4	14.9	15.5	21.3	25.1	29.6	25.9	22.4	19.0
Kutztown	76.1	86.9	91.2	90.8	88.2	85.4	85.0	83.2	81.9
Lock Haven	14.2	15.2	18.3	21.3	25.2	24.7	24.2	22.7	21.3
Mansfield	36.9	33.0	33.1	33.8	34.7	32.4	30.5	29.3	28.0
Millersville	20.1	21.8	24.1	31.2	39.2	43.2	42.6	40.1	38.7
Shippensburg	22.8	28.1	32.9	37.3	40.9	43.8	43.5	40.4	37.5
Slippery Rock	8.7	10.8	15.5	24.4	32.2	37.3	36.3	32.1	28.8
West Chester	31.9	32.8	32.4	30.5	31.2	31.9	31.0	28.1	24.4

SOURCE: National Center for Education Statistics, undated.

Table B.13. Faculty Contract Provisions, Pennsylvania and Selected Other States

Location	Faculty Compensation	Online Learning	Adjunct Faculty Compensation	Retrenchment
Pennsylvania (State System)	The salaries payable to faculty members is set forth in the pay schedule specified in the contract (Article 22.)	Except where specifically stated in a letter of appointment for a faculty member describing his or her job expectations, teaching through distance education technologies shall be voluntary. (Article 41)	Part-time ACADEMIC FACULTY MEMBERS [Adjuncts] shall be paid on the basis of one twenty-fourth (1/24) of a full-time academic year's salary for each workload hour taught. (Article 22)	When in the opinion of the STATE SYSTEM/UNIVERSITIES retrenchment becomes necessary and it cannot be accomplished totally by attrition, APSCUF and the affected FACULTY MEMBERS shall be notified prior to implementation, in accordance with the schedule set forth in Section F of this Article, and retrenchment shall be made as circumstances require, provided that the following order shall be utilized to the extent feasible in the department where retrenchment is occurring: a. temporary, part-time b. temporary, full-time c. regular, part-time d. regular, full-time Retrenchment shall be made in inverse order of length of service from the most recent date of employment at the University ("seniority"), within a department, provided the remaining ACADEMIC FACULTY MEMBERS have the necessary qualifications to teach the remaining courses or perform the remaining duties. ACADEMIC FACULTY MEMBERS shall be responsible for keeping their Academic Dean informed of all their qualifications (Article 29).

Location	Faculty Compensation	Online Learning	Adjunct Faculty Compensation	Retrenchment
California (California State)	Employees can be paid any amount on the schedule based on their rank and classification. The president can grant a salary increase to a probationary or tenured faculty unit member based on market conditions (Article 31).	In the assignment of workload, consideration shall be given at least to the following factors: graduate instruction; online instruction; activity classes; laboratory courses; supervision; distance learning; sports; and directed study. Consideration for adjustments in workload shall be given to at least the following: class size or number of students; course and curricular redesign; preparation for substantive changes in instructional methods, including development of online and hybrid courses (Article 20).	N/A	The order of layoff within a unit of layoff designated by the President for a reduction in force shall be: a. first, less than full-time temporary faculty unit employees who do not hold a three-year (or longer) appointment; b. next, full-time temporary faculty unit employees who do not hold a three-year (or longer) appointment; c. next, less than full-time temporary faculty unit employees who hold a three-year (or longer) appointment; d. next, full-time temporary faculty unit employees who hold a three-year (or longer) appointment; e. next, faculty in the Faculty Early Retirement Program; f. next, probationary faculty unit employees; g. last, tenured faculty unit employees (Article 35).

Location	Faculty Compensation	Online Learning	Adjunct Faculty Compensation	Retrenchment
New York (State University of New York)	Stipends for some geographic areas are available (Articles 20 and 25).	N/A	A part-time employee is paid on the basis of a prorated basic annual salary, which shall be the appropriately prorated amount of the minimum basic salary that would have been paid to the employee had the employee been employed on a full-time basis (Article 20).	Chancellor shall apply retrenchment among employees holding the position subject to retrenchment at such level of organization in inverse order of appointment within each affected group of employees hereinafter referred to as follows: 1. part-time employees holding term appointments before full-time employees holding term appointments. 2. full-time academic employees holding term appointments before academic employees holding continuing appointments. 3. part-time academic employees holding continuing appointments before full-time academics holding continuing appointments. 4. full-time professional employees holding term appointments before professional employees holding permanent appointments. 5. part-time professional employees holding permanent appointments before full-time professional employees holding permanent appointments (Article 35).

Location	Faculty Compensation	Online Learning	Adjunct Faculty Compensation	Retrenchment
New Jersey (state colleges and universities)	The College/ University can, at its discretion, hire faculty at any step of any salary range associated with any academic rank (Article 21).	In the event that an existing online course is to be revised, the employee shall receive an alternate assignment within load to revise the course if the Provost/Vice President for Academic Affairs determines that the extent of necessary revision so warrants. Employees shall be compensated for teaching online courses at the same rate that they are compensated for teaching the course on campus. Employees teaching an online course for the first time shall receive one additional credit, which is a one (1) time payment only (Article 34).	Adjunct faculty are paid on a separate scale under a separate adjunct agreement	To the extent that it is not inconsistent with the preservation of the institution's academic integrity and educational purpose, layoffs within a layoff unit shall be made in order of years of service, laying off employees with the fewest years of service first (Article 41).

Location	Faculty Compensation	Online Learning	Adjunct Faculty Compensation	Retrenchment

Maine (University of Maine System)	Universities have discretion subject to minimum salaries for each academic rank (Article 20).	Unit members will not be required to teach in ITV programs except when consistent with terms contained in letters of appointment (Article 12).	Unit members shall be assigned the appropriate rate of pay by the University for each assignment (based on credit hour rates) (Article 19).	1. For retrenchment within designated units, there shall be the following retrenchment categories:
				  a. less than one (1) year of employment
				  b. one (1) to three (3) years of employment
				  c. four (4) to six (6) years of employment
				  d. seven (7) to ten (10) years of employment
				  e. eleven (11) to fifteen (15) years of employment
				  f. sixteen (16) to twenty-one (21) years of employment
				  g. more than twenty-one (21) years of employment
				2. No tenured unit member shall be retrenched if there are nontenured unit members in the retrenchment unit.
				3. No unit member with a continuing contract shall be retrenched if there are unit members without a continuing contract in the retrenchment unit.
				4. Where unit members are equally qualified under 1 through 3 above, unit members will be retained whose qualifications are most essential to the mission and purpose of the retrenched unit (Article 17).

SOURCES: Association of Pennsylvania State College and University Faculties and the Pennsylvania State System of Higher Education, 2013; United University Professors and the State of New York, 2013; University of Maine System and Associated Faculties of the Universities of Maine, MEA/NEA, 2008; University of Maine System and the Maine Part-Time Faculty Association (undated), State of New Jersey and Council of New Jersey State College Locals, 2017; California Faculty Association and the Board of Trustees of the California State University, 2014.

Appendix C

Response of the State System's Interim Chancellor

Pennsylvania's
STATE SYSTEM
of Higher Education

OFFICE OF THE CHANCELLOR

April 12, 2018

Patricia Berger, Executive Director
Legislative Budget & Finance Committee
Room 400A, Finance Building
613 North Street
P.O. Box 8737
Harrisburg, PA 17105

RE: RAND Corporation report pursuant to SR 34 (Argall)

Dear Ms. Berger:

This letter is in response to your April 4, 2018 invitation to review the RAND Corporation's confidential draft report titled *Promoting the Long-Term Sustainability and Viability of Universities in the Pennsylvania State System of Higher Education.* Thank you for the opportunity to provide input.

The draft RAND report highlights internal and external challenges affecting higher education, in general, and Pennsylvania's State System of Higher Education (State System), in particular. The report also suggests various restructuring options, including considerations for implementation.

We are appreciative that RAND included an examination of our own *Strategic System Review* report as part of its study. Our top-to-bottom strategic review, which included input from hundreds of students, faculty, staff, university and System leaders, legislators, and community leaders, has since been guiding the State System's redesign efforts. So much so, the Board of Governors established three priorities:

☐ Ensuring student success
☐ Leveraging university strengths
☐ Transforming the governance/leadership structure.

We have made progress toward redesigning the System to be less bureaucratic and more student-focused. Already within the first six months of the process, we have affirmed a mission statement for student success; eliminated out-of-date and burdensome Board policies (regulations); and streamlined the processes for academic program approval, facilities planning, and real property acquisition/disposal. University efforts to better align academic program offerings with regional workforce needs are continuing to result in important changes. We also are working to enhance university flexibility, to align and achieve regional affordability through strategic pricing efforts, and to develop a more successful approach to collaborative procurement to capitalize on more strategic sourcing opportunities.

2986 N. Second Street, Harrisburg, PA 17110-1201 | 717.720.4000 | www.passhe.edu   **14 universities. Infinite opportunities.**

74

Through this lens, we reviewed the RAND Corporation draft report. That is, we reviewed the report to the extent to which it would impact students, enhance the efficiency and effectiveness of the State System and its member universities, and ensure strategic changes that support the State System's long-term success.

While we are pleased that the RAND study affirms many of the findings contained within our own strategic review report, we have serious concerns about the adverse impact several of the study's recommended options could have on students, specifically related to both affordability and access.

The report acknowledges that if the State System universities either were placed under the control of a state-related university (Option 4) or merged into the state-related university structure (Option 5), it is possible—even likely—that tuition and fee rates "would rise to levels similar to the state-related branch campuses, potentially worsening affordability for Pennsylvania families."

The same result could occur in Option 3, in which at least some of the State System universities would become state-related. (The current average in-state tuition rate of $7,974 charged in the State System is less than half that charged by either Pennsylvania State University or the University of Pittsburgh.)

Access also could be negatively impacted if the State System universities either were placed under the control of a state-related university or subsumed entirely as recommended in Options 4 and 5, respectively. Such changes "would likely result in reduction in the current mission at some or all of the current State System universities as they are merged into the state-related system or systems," the report states.

Overall, while none of the recommended options contained in the RAND study would result in any guaranteed savings for the universities or the Commonwealth, Options 3, 4, and 5 likely would result in higher costs and fewer options for students—certainly not outcomes anyone would want to see. These options may also increase university financial risk and may eliminate the defense that sovereign immunity affords at present.

It is important to note that the demographic challenges currently affecting a majority of the State System universities are having the same impact on nearly all of Penn State's branch campuses ("Commonwealth Campuses") and the University of Pittsburgh's branch campuses. According to publically available data, 15 of Penn State's 19 Commonwealth Campuses have fewer students enrolled today than they did in 2010, while all four of Pitt's branch campuses have fewer students than they did during the same time.

The primary factor affecting enrollment in all sectors of higher education in the state—public and private—is the state's changing demographics, which is resulting in a smaller number of high school graduates each year. As a result, a large majority of the four-year, degree-granting institutions in Pennsylvania—both public and private—have experienced enrollment declines in recent years, a fact confirmed by data submitted annually to the National Center for Education Statistics through the Integrated Postsecondary Education Data System (IPEDS). This is a trend that is expected to continue for at least several more years.

Despite the changing demographics, 10 of our universities are among the Top 25 largest universities in Pennsylvania. Nearly 90 percent of our students are Pennsylvania residents; most will remain here after they graduate. And, our graduation rates exceed the national average among similar, comprehensive, public universities.

Shifting control of the State System universities to the state-related institutions will not change the factors affecting enrollment. Nor would it address the other major factor affecting the universities' long-term sustainability—lagging state support. As has been noted in other forums, prior to the last three years, the State System experienced seven consecutive years of either reduced or level funding from the state, including a $90 million reduction in one year, resulting in this year's appropriation approximating the amount received in 2002—16 years ago.

As our System Redesign proceeds, we must keep focus on what really matters to students and their families—affordability and access—as well as relevant academic programs. We must create additional academic opportunities that prepare students for success in their lives and careers in Pennsylvania's global society. Implementing organizational changes that could have significant detrimental impact on students with identified disadvantages is not the answer.

It would be ill-advised to hastily implement drastic options that could harm students, without allowing the State System an appropriate opportunity to fully realize the outcomes of our strategic, intentional, and thoughtful System Redesign efforts.

The Board of Governors, the Office of the Chancellor, and the universities are committed to the long-term success of each and every one of our 14 universities. Working together with our students, faculty, staff and other stakeholders, we are redesigning the System for the future and welcome the opportunity to continue the discussion of these important issues, which are vital not only to the future of the State System, but also to the future of the Commonwealth.

Sincerely,

Karen M. Whitney, Ph.D.
Interim Chancellor

cc: Jennifer Hoover, Director of Governmental Relations

References

Act 188—*See* Commonwealth of Pennsylvania Office of the Budget.

Association of Pennsylvania State College and University Faculties and the Pennsylvania State System of Higher Education, "Agreement Between Association of Pennsylvania State College and University Faculties (APSCUF) and the Pennsylvania State System of Higher Education (State System), July 21, 2015, to June 30, 2018," June 2013. As of March 28, 2018:
http://www.apscuf.org/contracts/APSCUFfacultyCBA2015-18.pdf

Bransberger, Peace, and Demarée K. Michelau, *Knocking at the College Door: Projections of High School Graduates*, 9th ed., Boulder, Colo.: Western Interstate Commission for Higher Education, December 2016. As of April 11, 2018:
http://www.wiche.edu/knocking

California Faculty Association and the Board of Trustees of the California State University, "Collective Bargaining Agreement Between the California Faculty Association and the Board of Trustees of the California State University Unit 3: Faculty, Ratified November 12, 2014, in Effect Until June 30, 2017," 2014. As of March 28, 2018:
https://www.calfac.org/sites/main/files/file-attachments/cfa_cba_2014-17_final_1.23.2015.pdf

Commonwealth of Pennsylvania, Act 188: 24 P.S. §20-2001-A et seq. (as amended through July 6, 2016). As of March 18, 2018:
http://www.passhe.edu/inside/legal/documents/act188.pdf

Commonwealth of Pennsylvania Office of the Budget, Commonwealth Budget, 2018–19 Proposed Budget [and earlier editions], February 6, 2018. As of April 13, 2018:
http://www.budget.pa.gov/PublicationsAndReports/CommonwealthBudget/Pages/default.aspx

Faust, Janine, "Pitt Board of Trustees Endorses Titusville Training Hub," *Pitt News*, February 26, 2018. As of March 18, 2018:
https://pittnews.com/article/128249/top-stories/pitt-board-trustees-endorses-titusville-campus-training-hub/

Gardner, Lee, "Georgia's Mergers Offer Lessons, and Cautions, to Other States," *Chronicle of Higher Education*, June 19, 2017. As of March 18, 2018:
https://www.chronicle.com/article/Georgia-s-Mergers-Offer/240390

Gardner, Lee, "How Maine Became a Laboratory for the Future of Public Higher Ed," *Chronicle of Higher Education*, February 25, 2018. As of March 18, 2018:
https://www.chronicle.com/article/How-Maine-Became-a-Laboratory/242621

General Assembly of Pennsylvania, Senate Resolution No. 34, resolution directing the Legislative Budget and Finance Committee to conduct a study and issue a report relating to the long-term sustainability and viability of the Pennsylvania State System of Higher Education, 2017. As of April 13, 2018:
http://www.legis.state.pa.us/CFDOCS/Legis/PN/Public/btCheck.cfm?txtType=HTM&sessYr=2017&sessInd=0&billBody=S&billTyp=R&billNbr=0034&pn=0624

Moody's Investor Services, "Higher Education Rating Methodology," December 21, 2017. As of March 14, 2018 (available with site registration):
http://www.moodys.com/researchdocumentcontentpage.aspx?docid=PBC_1106425

National Center for Education Statistics, *Integrated Postsecondary Data System*, undated. As of March 14, 2018:
https://nces.ed.gov/ipeds/

National Center for Higher Education Management Systems, *Pennsylvania State System of Higher Education Strategic System Review Findings and Recommendations*, Boulder, Colo., July 12, 2017. As of March 14, 2018:
http://www.passhe.edu/systemreview/pages/default.aspx

NCHEMS—*See* National Center for Higher Education Management Systems.

New York State, "Tuition-Free Degree Program: The Excelsior Scholarship," undated. As of March 28, 2018:
https://www.ny.gov/programs/tuition-free-degree-program-excelsior-scholarship

Pennsylvania State Data Center, *State and County Population Projections by Age and Gender, Pennsylvania: 2010 to 2040*, Middletown, Pa., 2012.

Quinton, Sophie, "Merging Colleges to Cut Costs and Still Boost Graduation Rates," *Stateline*, March 29, 2017. As of April 13, 2018:
http://www.pewtrusts.org/en/research-and-analysis/blogs/stateline/2017/03/29/merging-colleges-to-cut-costs-and-still-boost-graduation-rates

State of New Jersey and Council of New Jersey State College Locals, "Agreement: State of New Jersey, Council of New Jersey State College Locals, AFT, AFL-CIO, State College/Universities Unit, July 1, 2015–June 30, 2019," October 2017. As of March 28, 2018:
http://www.cnjscl.org/AFT%20FT%202015-2019%20final%20contract.pdf

United University Professors and the State of New York, "Agreement Between United University Professors and the State of New York, July 2, 1011–July 1, 2016," June 2013. As of March 28, 2018:
http://uupinfo.org/negotiations/Contract2011to2016webSECUREv9.pdf

University of Maine System and Associated Faculties of the Universities of Maine, "Agreement Between University of Maine System and Associated Faculties of the Universities of Maine, MEA/NEA, 2015–2017," May 2008. As of March 28, 2018:
http://staticweb.maine.edu/wp-content/uploads/2013/08/AFUM_2015-2017.pdf?ca0c38

University of Maine System and the Maine Part-Time Faculty Association, "Agreement Between University of Maine System and the Maine Part-Time Faculty Association, American Federation of Teachers Local #4593, AFT-Maine, AFL-CIO, September 1, 2015–August 31, 2017," undated. As of March 28, 2018:
http://staticweb.maine.edu/wp-content/uploads/2016/05/PATFA-contract-2015-2017.pdf?ca0c38